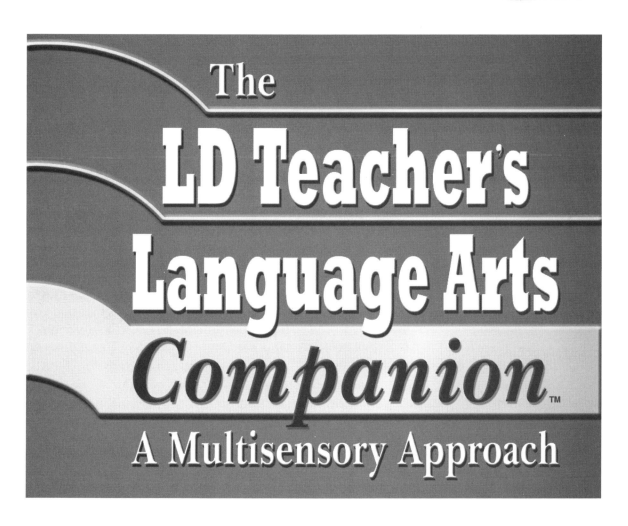

The LD Teacher's Language Arts *Companion*™

A Multisensory Approach

Elizabeth M. Wadlington
Paula S. Currie

LinguiSystems, Inc.
3100 4th Avenue
East Moline, IL 61244-9700

1-800-PRO IDEA
1-800-776-4332

Skill:	Language Arts
Ages:	8-15
Grades:	3-10

FAX: 1-800-577-4555
E-mail: service@linguisystems.com
Web: www.linguisystems.com

TDD: 1-800-933-8331
(for those with hearing impairments)

Printed in the U.S.A.
ISBN 0-7606-0468-1

About the Authors

Paula S. Currie, Ph.D., is an Associate Professor and Head of the Department of Communication Sciences & Disorders at Southeastern Louisiana University (SLU) in Hammond, LA. Dr. Currie is also the Program Director for the undergraduate and graduate programs in speech-language pathology at SLU. She teaches courses in assessment and treatment of communication and learning disorders, and has developed and teaches a course about language and literacy. Dr. Currie has extensive experience diagnosing and treating individuals with communication disorders. She has worked in public school, private practice, hospital, and university settings. She serves as a consultant to Louisiana's Assistive Technical Network. She lives in Ponchatoula, LA, with her husband, Mark, and her two sons, Taylor and Zachary. This is her fourth book with LinguiSystems. She is a co-author of *125 Ways to Be a Better Student*. She also co-authored *125 Ways to Be a Better Reader* and *The Source for Learning Disabilities* with Elizabeth Wadlington.

Elizabeth M. Wadlington, Ph.D., is a Professor in the Department of Teaching and Learning at Southeastern Louisiana University (SLU) in Hammond, LA. Her responsibilities include graduate and undergraduate courses in reading, elementary education, and early childhood education. She has a special interest in learning difficulties because her own son has struggled and coped successfully with dyslexia. As a result, she is actively involved in consultation, assessment, and teaching those with reading problems. She has also served on numerous committees and boards to develop and implement learning and teaching improvements. In addition, she has had many journal articles published and has presented at national/international conferences. Prior to coming to SLU, Elizabeth taught kindergarten and elementary school, trained and assessed Head Start teachers, and worked in adult literacy. She currently lives in Mandeville, LA, with her husband, Charles. This is her third book with LinguiSystems. She also co-authored *125 Ways to Be a Better Reader* and *The Source for Learning Disabilities* with Paula Currie.

Dedications

Paula: to all of the people with learning disabilities and to the colleagues and individuals with whom I have worked

Beth: with love and gratitude to Charles and Patrick

Table of Contents

Table of Contents, *continued*

1 Introduction

This book is for teachers, parents, speech-language pathologists, and other professionals who care deeply about students who have learning disabilities and want to help them. It is also written for the students themselves who, with or without assistance, can implement the activities. For the sake of clarity, we have directed the language to teachers; however, others will be able to adapt the activities to fit their settings and special needs.

Before we can begin to discuss ways to help students with learning disabilities, we must first define the term *learning disability*. Unfortunately, there is no definition that is agreed upon by everyone in the field. For this book, we have chosen to use the definition below as provided by the Individuals with Disabilities Education Act (IDEA) (PL 101-476, 1997).

Definition

Learning Disability is a disorder of one or more of the basic psychological processes involved in understanding or using spoken or written language, which may manifest itself in an imperfect ability to listen, think, speak, read, write, spell, or to do mathematical calculations.

The National Center for Learning Disabilities (1997) goes on to state that learning disability is a neurological disorder that interferes with an individual's ability to store, process, or produce information. People with learning disabilities do not perform up to the level of their abilities or intelligence. Learning disabilities *do not* include difficulties that are the result of physical problems (visual, hearing, or motor); mental retardation; emotional disturbances; or environmental, cultural, and economic factors (IDEA, 1997).

It is important to remember that students with learning disabilities are all different. Some people with learning disabilities have many difficulties; others have only a few. These difficulties are sometimes mild or moderate; other times, they are severe. Therefore, no single method, curriculum, or program will be effective for all students with learning disabilities. It is critical to know the specific characteristics of students and tailor instruction to meet their particular needs.

Although needs are diverse, approximately 85% of children with learning disabilities have some type of problem with expressive and/or receptive language (Lyon, 1996).

When students have problems with language, all areas of the curriculum, as well as personal attitudes and social skills, are affected. Special activities are needed to help these students succeed. We have developed the multisensory activities in this book to do just that.

Multisensory Instruction

Multisensory instruction involves multiple senses as well as movement. Many students, especially those with learning disabilities, learn best when they send learning to the brain along multiple pathways. Therefore, structured activities that involve auditory, visual, tactile, and kinesthetic learning are desirable when teaching these students. The students themselves can also be trained to use multisensory strategies when studying, doing homework, and learning new skills.

Multisensory learning can be noisier and take more time than traditional learning. You may find you need to modify or change your instructional environment to make multisensory learning possible. It also may be necessary to educate those who think that learning can only take place when students are quiet, still, and seated at their desks. Fortunately, most students, both those with and those without learning disabilities, enjoy and benefit from multisensory activities. Because most students respond to multisensory instruction, teachers can use those approaches with the whole class rather than just with students with learning disabilities.

Frequently, kinesthetic and tactile learners are left behind in the classroom because most teaching situations are set up for auditory and visual learners only. All too often, schools wait for children to fail before they become serious about helping them. We want to encourage educators and parents to begin using multisensory activities and other interventions at the first sign of difficulty. We encourage you to experiment with different intervention approaches and analyze why some work and others do not. Ask students for suggestions to make instruction more meaningful. As a result, activities that are a good fit for students can be used without wasting time on meaningless or frustrating activities.

English/Language Arts Standards

To make it easier for teachers to meet accountability expectations, we have referenced the activities in this book to the English/Language Arts Standards developed by the International Reading Association (IRA) and National Council of Teachers of English (NCTE) (1996). These standards are an outgrowth of real classroom practices; however, they are not a prescription for teaching language arts. Rather, they are a listing of what students should know and be able to do. They are intended to be suggestive, but not an exhaustive resource of good language arts practices. They are meant to be used as starting points for ongoing dialog about curriculum and activities.

The twelve English/Language Arts Standards are listed on the following page. The standards are not written in a hierarchy but are only numbered for ease of reference. They overlap with each other, and there are complex relationships among them. Most teaching and learning activities in this book will address several of them simultaneously.

6

1 Students read a wide range of print and nonprint texts to build an understanding of texts, of themselves, and of the cultures of the United States and the world. They also read to acquire new information, to respond to the needs and demands of society and the workplace, and for personal fulfillment. Among these texts are fiction and nonfiction, classic, and contemporary works.

2 Students read a wide range of literature from many periods in many genres to build an understanding of the many dimensions (philosophical, ethical, aesthetic) of human experience.

3 Students apply a wide range of strategies to comprehend, interpret, evaluate, and appreciate texts. They draw on their prior experience, their interactions with other readers and writers, their knowledge of word meaning and of other texts, their word identification strategies, and their understanding of textual features (sound-letter correspondence, sentence structure, context, graphics).

4 Students adjust their use of spoken, written, and visual language (conventions, style, vocabulary) to communicate effectively with a variety of audiences and for different purposes.

5 Students employ a wide range of strategies as they write and use different writing process elements appropriately to communicate with different audiences for a variety of purposes.

6 Students apply knowledge of language structure, language conventions (spelling and punctuation), media techniques, figurative language, and genre to create, critique, and discuss print and nonprint texts.

7 Students conduct research on issues and interests by generating ideas and questions, and by posing problems. They gather, evaluate, and synthesize data from a variety of sources (print and nonprint texts, artifacts, people) to communicate their discoveries in ways that suit their purpose and audience.

8 Students use a variety of technological and information resources (libraries, databases, computer networks, video) to gather and synthesize information and to create and communicate knowledge.

9 Students develop an understanding of and respect for diversity in language use, patterns, and dialects across cultures, ethnic groups, geographic regions, and social roles.

10 Students whose first language is not English make use of their first language to develop competency in the English language arts and to develop understanding of content across the curriculum.

11 Students participate as knowledgeable, reflective, creative, and critical members of a variety of literacy communities.

12 Students use spoken, written, and visual language to accomplish their own purposes (for learning, enjoyment, persuasion, and the exchange of information).

How to Use This Book

For Teachers and Other Professionals

The ways to use multisensory instruction are endless. We feel that we have only touched the tip of the iceberg with the ones included in this book. It was very hard to choose which activities to include and which ones to leave out. We decided to focus on activities that take a minimum of teacher preparation and are easily understood by students. We have also tried to incorporate as many different modalities into each activity as seems practical. We encourage you to use the ideas in this book only as beginning points and to adapt or extend them to fit the individual needs of your students. Students can often offer valuable insights as to what works, what does not work, and how to modify activities to be more effective.

A few activities found in different chapters are somewhat similar but have different purposes. You can use these separately or together to best fit your students and circumstances.

Although, the English/Language Arts Standards are not meant to be distinct and separable from each other, many school districts now require teachers to reference their lesson plans to individual standards. For this reason, we have forced a separation and referenced the multisensory activities to individual standards. We want to emphasize that this book is an "activity" book that has been referenced to the standards rather than a "standards" book with activities designed specifically to support each standard. For ease of use, we have included the number of the standard(s) most clearly represented after each activity. We have also cross-referenced activities to related standards in the **Standards Matrix** in the Appendix on page 141.

Notice that Standard 10 deals with students whose first language is not English. Multisensory activities are very good for these students because using multiple senses and movement allows them to overcome language barriers to learn English language arts and content across curriculum. It also provides them with a variety of formats to demonstrate their knowledge and skills. You can make use of the first language of each of these students as well as English as you facilitate the activities.

Although we have referenced activities to the standards that they most clearly address from our perspective, each activity can be related to many more. We are aware that teachers and students may use activities in their own unique ways and focus on standards we did not reference. Therefore, we encourage readers to correlate the activities to other standards as appropriate for their own situations.

At the beginning of each chapter, we have included general goals for the activities contained in it. Use these in your planning, but feel free to write more specific goals depending upon your students' individual strengths and weaknesses.

Use the **Action Plan** on page 10 to plan ways to meet student needs, work toward IEP goals, show accountability, get ready for parent conferences, and so forth. This sheet is designed to record long-range plans for learning; however, it can easily be modified for daily use (include daily objectives after long-range goals; limit timeline to one day; make other modifications required by school system). Plans usually work better if teachers and parents collaborate to develop and implement them. You will find a sample completed **Action Plan** on page 11.

For Parents

This book can be used by parents to effectively work with their own children. Parents may want to begin by identifying the learning modality preferences of their children. The **Learning Styles Inventory** on page 23 is a good starting place. Parents can also observe their children over a short period of time and keep notes as to techniques used to successfully learn new skills and their degree of success.

The **Action Plan** discussed earlier for classroom use can be modified to be used by parents at home. Although many goals for school and home will be the same, parents can also set goals unique to the home situation. Examples of home goals include using good telephone manners, memorizing steps for doing the laundry, and things to remember when babysitting a sibling.

Although all chapters can be very beneficial to parents, Chapter 8, beginning on page 121, emphasizes the important role parents play in their children's development of language and literacy. It is filled with background information, suggestions, and activities that parents need to help their children learn. It tells parents how to work with educators and other professionals collaboratively to set goals and plan interventions. It also gives some websites to which parents can refer to get more information. Recognizing that many children go to day care and early intervention programs, the activities in Chapter 8 are also useful for early interventionists and childcare providers.

Beth & Paula

9

Action Plan

Student:			Date:	

Check areas that apply:	____ Home	____ School	____ Specific Class:

Standards to Emphasize:	

Goals:	

Timeline:	

Materials

Multisensory Activities

Other Accommodations/Modifications or Special Needs

Assessment Techniques

Success of Plan

Action Plan

Student: *Rosita Gomez*		Date: *4/4*	

Check areas that apply:	✓ Home	✓ School	✓ Specific Class: *Social Studies*

Standards to Emphasize:	*English/Language Arts 7, 10, 12*
Goals:	*To appreciate her history*
	To use different resources to research her family history
	To develop competence in English and native Spanish
	To express her findings in a creative way
Timeline:	*Due on 4/19*

Materials

family members (especially grandmother), Internet, family tree, books from school library, art materials of her choice

Multisensory Activities

Base this on Activity M1 but encourage Rosita to express her findings in her own unique way (M12) and to use Spanish to communicate with her older family members.

Other Accommodations/Modifications or Special Needs

Rosita will need a ride to her grandmother's house after school. She will need to be able to use the Internet at school. She will need step-by-step visual and auditory directions for using Internet search engines.

Assessment Techniques

Observation of student work habits; finished product

Success of Plan

Rosita wrote a very creative poem about her history and illustrated it on a timeline of which she was very proud. Her English vocabulary, grammar, and spelling were good. She explained the Spanish vocabulary of her older relatives. She needs a little more practice in using Internet search engines.

References

Currie, P. & Wadlington, E. (2000). *The source for learning disabilities.* East Moline, IL: LinguiSystems.

Lyon, G. Learning Disabilities: Special education for students with disabilities (1996, Spring). *The Future of Children,* 6(1).

National Center for Learning Disabilities (1997). Information about learning disabilities. Retrieved May 22, 2001, from http://www.ncld.org/ld.info_ld.html.

National Council of Teachers of English & International Reading Association (1996). *Standards for the English language arts.*

Council for Exceptional Children (1999, April/May). Primer on IDEA 1997 and its regulations. *CEC Today: Newsletter of the Council for Exceptional Children,* 5(7).

Wadlington, E. & Currie, P. (2000). *125 ways to be a better reader.* East Moline, IL: LinguiSystems.

2 Motivation

Students with learning disabilities have often experienced failure in both school and everyday life. Because of those failures, they sometimes give up on learning at an early age. Effective teachers know that before they can teach these students, they have to help students build realistic self-concepts, develop positive self-esteem, and view themselves as capable learners. Teachers also must find out students' interests and build upon them. In addition, they need to understand the source of poor attitudes so they can help students change them.

To become competent in spoken, written, and visual language and use it for their own purposes (Standard 12), students must first be motivated to learn. They need to want to pay attention and strive to do their best. The activities in this section were designed to help students become self-aware and help teachers get to know their students and inspire them to understand and use the language arts effectively.

Goals

- To develop and appreciate a sense of self
- To appreciate similarities and differences among individuals
- To build self-esteem
- To find an area of excellence
- To remove barriers to learning
- To replace negative attitudes with positive ones
- To identify one's learning style preferences
- To adjust use of modalities to meet special needs
- To become competent in self-expression
- To use language for different purposes
- To do one's best

| M1 | ## My Life Timeline | Standards: 7, 11, 12 |

Students need to develop a sense of themselves as individuals with unique histories, strengths, and weaknesses. To help your students develop a sense of personal history, have them develop timelines of their own lives. Give them large note cards or pieces of colored paper on which to write and/or illustrate important events in their lives. Events such as the following can be used:

- The day I was born
- My first pet
- My first day of school
- My favorite vacation
- My most memorable birthday
- A day that changed my life

Some students may want to take this activity a step farther by collaborating with their families to use resources such as relatives, family trees, and diaries to find out about their ancestors. Post the timelines around the room and let students view and discuss each other's timelines.

| *I was born in Mexico City.* | *We moved to the U.S. when I was in first grade.* | *I read my first English book by myself in second grade.* | *¡Hola! In fourth grade, we visited our relatives in Mexico.* | *I made our school soccer team in sixth grade.* |

| M2 | ## All About Me! | Standards: 8, 12 |

Students are more likely to try their best when they know the teacher is interested in them, their feelings, and their preferences. Use this activity to find out about your students' interests, attitudes, and values. At the beginning of the school year, have your students draw/paint and cut/paste from magazines and the Internet to make "All About Me!" booklets. Allow them to use puffy paint, colored glue, or other textured materials to write text in their booklets. Let your students share their books with you, each other, and their parents. Depending on the ages of the students, pages can include topics listed on the next page.

- What I like about myself
- What I do best
- My favorite thing to do at school
- My favorite thing to do at home
- My friends
- My biggest success
- My biggest problem
- My hero

| M3 | Sentence Starters | Standard: 12 |

Some students have problems thinking of ideas to illustrate in booklets like the one described in Activity **M2**. Providing students with sentence starters will help them generate some of their own ideas. Rather than just writing the rest of the sentence, ask your students to draw or act it out. Some examples of sentence starters include:

- If I inherited a million dollars today, I would . . .
- If I could have been born in a different time and place, I would . . .
- If I could see into the future, I might . . .
- If I were an animal, I would be . . .
- If my teacher (parents) only knew . . .
- I could be a better person if . . .
- My secret is . . .
- I wish my teacher (or mom or dad) would . . .
- If I were an author, I would . . .
- If I were President of the United States, I would . . .
- If I could invent a new language, it would . . .

| M4 | Me Collages | Standards: 8, 11, 12 |

Ask students to brainstorm character traits that fit themselves. If they have trouble getting started, give them a list of character traits from which to choose (joyful, sad, honest, intelligent, trustworthy, kind). Let them add to the list as they think of others. Then have them collect and cut pictures from magazines, newspapers, and the Internet to make collages that express their unique personalities. Encourage students to create descriptive titles (*Slugger Steve, Laughing Latasha, Moody Miriam, Patient Paula*) for their collages. If they display one set of character traits in one situation, such as on the playground, and other traits in another one, such as at home, let them divide their collages into sections, with each section representing a different situation. Discuss why people act differently in different settings and how to know the real person. Have students compare their collages and discuss similarities and difference among individuals.

| M5 | **Interest Charades** | Standard: 12 |

Most students like to play "Charades." Rather than acting out movie or book titles, though, have students dramatize their interests and hobbies. Some activities your students might pantomime include painting, playing soccer, or playing the piano. Take notes about their interests so you can use them as themes for later projects. Note your students' preferences so you can motivate shy, discouraged, or non-responsive children to participate in learning activities.

| M6 | **An Area of Excellence** | Standards: 7, 12 |

Students with disabilities are more likely to be successful in school and life if they have an area in which to excel. Some children just naturally develop their talents; others need help to find them. Begin by talking about your personal experiences (your weaknesses, your area of excellence, struggles to succeed, positive and negative emotions, etc.). Then ask students to share and brainstorm a list of areas of excellence. Write their responses on the board. Be sure to include a wide range of talents (baseball, computers, art, pet sitting, making others feel good about themselves, creative thinking). Through discussion and modeling, help students to value all areas of excellence. Later, have students research their areas of excellence in books and on the Internet. Let them illustrate or write about their special areas. Post their illustrations and written work on an "Excellence" bulletin board.

| M7 | **Good Things** | Standards: 11, 12 |

Because many students with learning disabilities have had unpleasant experiences at school, they have a tendency to be negative about school and learning in general. Even when good things happen to them at school, they are apt to see their glasses as half empty rather than half full. You can help these children begin to change their negative perceptions.

First, consider the school day from a student's perspective. Ask yourself questions like these:
- Is the school day stress-free?
- Are there opportunities for everyone to succeed?
- Do I individualize as needed?
- Do all students frequently receive positive recognition for something?
- Are there some students who seem to receive mostly negative attention?
- Am I modeling positive behaviors?
- Do I purposely state ideas in a positive manner whenever possible?
- Am I open to new ways of doing things?

After reflection, make changes in the school environment as needed. Then at the end of each day, play a game in which students name or draw three good things that happened that day. Emphasize looking for the good in all situations. Let students share their "good things" with each other. Give a small reward to each student for looking on the bright side.

After students grow accustomed to this activity, it can be extended. Challenge students to make something good happen to someone else in the classroom each day.

Good Things That Happened Today
by Tremell

1. I had pancakes for breakfast.

2. I made a goal in soccer.

3. I understood the science work.

4. I sat by Dion at lunch.

| M8 | **Barriers to Learning** | Standard: 12 |

Removing barriers that may be holding students back will help them become better learners. Ask students to talk about situations and problems that keep them from learning. These could be intrinsic (attitude, motivation, lack of self-discipline) or extrinsic (no quiet place to study, too much work, no one to help with homework). Help students develop concrete plans to overcome the barriers. The **Barriers to Learning Plan** on page 21 will help students plan ways to overcome their barriers. Provide your students with copies of the plan and encourage them to complete it and follow it. A completed plan can be found on page 22 to use as a model.

| M9 | **Stress Reducers** | Standards: 2, 9, 10, 11, 12 |

A quick way to quench motivation is to allow stress to impede upon a learning situation. Make your classroom as stress-free as possible by implementing the following suggestions:
- Provide a positive climate.
- Be respectful of all cultures and teach your children to respect diversity.
- Build trust between yourself and students and among students.
- Provide instruction at appropriate levels for students.
- Plan activities that allow students to use diverse learning styles.
- Use multisensory techniques in your instruction.
- Help students see mistakes as learning opportunities.
- Make mistakes on purpose, call attention to them, and model appropriate reactions.
- Encourage kindness and cooperation.
- Do not tolerate teasing or bullying.
- Provide positive social interactions for all students including those students who are shy, fearful, passive, or aggressive.
- Make a special effort to include the needs of students whose first language is not English in all activities.

When students experience stress, have them participate in multisensory stress-reducers such as these:
- Role-play stressful situations with happy endings.
- Visualize and describe working through problems in successful ways.
- Help others solve their problems. (This takes students' minds off of their own stressors and makes them feel good about themselves.)
- Draw pictures depicting feelings.
- Participate in water play or painting to soothe nerves.
- Participate in exercise and movement activities to relieve stress.
- Communicate feelings through artwork, music, or journaling.
- Read and discuss literature in which characters experience stressful situations similar to those of your students.

| M10 | ## Attitude Adjustments | Standard: 12 |

When students with learning disabilities experience numerous failures, they sometimes develop poor attitudes toward learning. Even when they want to change their attitudes, they often fall back into negative ways of thinking. Follow these steps to show your students how to use visualization to overcome poor attitudes.

1. Ask students to be honest and admit if their attitudes need improvement.
2. Have students use construction paper, glue, and clay to make a symbol for one of their poor attitudes.
3. Have students make an attractive symbol for the new attitude they want to replace the poor one.
4. Have students "bust" their negative attitudes (crumple them up, rip them to pieces, pound them shapeless).
5. Have them attach the new attitude to a prominent place, such as the corner of the desk, a notebook, or a book bag.
6. Have students practice visualizing busting the negative attitude and replacing it with the positive one.
7. Encourage them to do this visualization technique any time they are tempted to have a bad attitude.

| M11 | ## Learning Styles | Standard: 12 |

Students learn better when they and their teachers recognize their individual learning styles. Use the **Learning Styles Inventory** on page 23 to help your students pinpoint the ways they learn best. Provide each student with an individual copy of the completed inventory. You might consider enlarging the inventory and posting it on a bulletin board in your room.

Whenever you give an assignment, have students use their own Learning Styles Inventory to figure out the best way to study. Help students understand that they are not locked into using only the senses they innately prefer. Although they will probably always have a definite preference, they often can develop under-used senses with practice and use these senses to learn content specific to them. For example, they might use auditory strategies for learning to speak a foreign language and visual ones for learning to draw.

Be aware that sometimes teachers unconscientiously teach to their own learning styles exclusively. To avoid this problem, you can use the inventory to identify your own learning style and be sure to effectively teach both students that learn in a manner similar to you and those that learn very differently from you.

M12	**How I Like to Express Myself**	Standards: 9, 10, 11, 12

Students are motivated by being allowed to express themselves in their own unique ways. Some use spoken language; others prefer written language. Many students like to express themselves through creative writing, art, drama, or dance. Some use multiple nonverbal gestures and facial expressions as they speak, while others don't. Some students speak in local dialect while others may have a dialect from a distant geographical region. Bilingual students may mix words from multiple languages. Most students communicate more formally when talking to a teacher about an assignment than they do when hanging out with friends after school.

To help students become aware of their own preferences, have them complete the **Self-Expression Activity** on page 24. Ask them to model their answers for the class. As they discuss self-expression with others, help them see how it can be beneficial to be able to express themselves in multiple ways. Encourage them to respect differences among classmates. As a follow-up, have bilingual students teach a few words or phrases from their native languages to the rest of the class.

M13	**Motivational Contracts**	Standard: 12

Students with learning disabilities frequently feel that they have no control over anything in their lives. If they fail, they assume it is because they are stupid. If they succeed, they attribute it to luck. Contracts are a way to help these students be aware that they have control over their futures and motivate them to do their best. Students should get to make choices (within limits) as they work with teachers to develop contracts. Contracts should always be renegotiable if they do not work. Students can keep their contracts in a place where they will see them often and should begin each day by reading them aloud. An example of a blank **Contract** you can use is on page 26. A completed contract is shown here. Note that a space is left at the top of the blank contract for students to insert their own artwork or clip art to personalize the agreement. For another example of the use of contracts, see activity **H9** on page 129.

Contract

I've got an offer you can't refuse!

If I do these things: *learn to read the script for the class play*

(pronouncing the words correctly and with expression)

On this timeline: *one-half by 10/7; one-half by 10/14*

Then I get to: *sing the opening song for the play*

Student *Mary Patel* Date *9/30*

Teacher *Mr. Patrick*

Barriers to Learning Plan

Name:	Date:

1. What keeps me from learning? _____
   _____
   _____
   _____
   _____
   _____

2. What's my plan? _____
   _____
   _____
   _____
   _____
   _____

3. What's my timeline? | Date began _____ | Date to check my plan _____

4. Is the plan working? Why or why not? _____
   _____
   _____
   _____
   _____
   _____

5. Do I need to make changes to my plan? Describe any changes. _____
   _____
   _____
   _____
   _____
   _____

Barriers to Learning Plan (completed)

Name: *Hakan*	Date: *3/11*

1. What keeps me from learning? *I don't have anyone to check my math because my mom works late.*

2. What's my plan? *I can ask my mom if I can leave my math paper out for her to check early the next morning. When she has to leave too early, Ms. Tate can check my paper before the bell rings, and I can make corrections during homeroom.*

3. What's my timeline? | Date began *3/11* | Date to check my plan *3/18*

4. Is the plan working? Why or why not? *Sometimes it works, but I don't have time to correct math during homeroom.*

5. Do I need to make changes to my plan? Describe any changes. *I'm going to correct my math in Ms. Tate's class before the bell rings.*

22

Learning Styles Inventory[1]

Check the statements that best describe what you most often do or say. When you finish, count the number of checks in each column and write the total in the box under each column. The column with the greatest number of checks will give you a clue about your learning style preference. Don't be surprised if you don't have a strong preference for one style over the others. Many of us learn in more than one way. Recognize the style you prefer most and use the information to help you learn.

Auditory	Visual	Tactile/Kinesthetic
I like to listen to discussions.	I like to read information.	I like to touch the materials used in the activity.
The way someone talks (loudness and pitch) helps me recognize important information.	Bold print and italicized words are important.	I collect objects like the ones in the activity I did or watched.
I listen to the directions to know what to do.	I read the directions to know what to do.	I "do" each step in the directions to understand better.
I study best in small group discussions.	I study by reading and rereading my books and notes.	Walking back and forth helps me concentrate when I study.
A tape recorder helps me remember.	When I see it, I remember it.	An activity at the end of the lesson helps me understand.
I use and create "sayings" to remember difficult or lengthy information.	I write things down to remember.	I read, write, and then reread and re-write my notes to remember.
I study by "going over it in my head."	I study by "seeing it in my mind."	I study by "practicing."
I like someone to "call it out to me" when I study.	I like to write it down when I study.	I like to "say it and write it" when I study.
Reading out loud helps me understand.	Reading silently helps me understand.	Reading and working "as I go along" helps me understand.
Noise bothers me when I read or study.	Too many words or pictures on the page confuse me.	I need "to do some" so I can understand.
Total number checked	Total number checked	Total number checked

[1]Wadlington, E. & Currie, P. *125 Ways to Be a Better Reader*. LinguiSystems: East Moline, IL, 2000.

23

Self-Expression

Name _____

Read each situation. Then write the letter of one or more of the ways you would express your thoughts and feelings in the blank. Explain why you chose the method of expression you did. If the way you would express yourself is not listed, choose "other" and describe the way you would express yourself. (Feel free to write more than one letter to combine modes of self-expression.)

a. casual spoken language	f. music
b. formal spoken language	g. art
c. casual written language	h. dance or movement
d. formal written language	i. creative writing/speaking
e. drama	j. other

_____ 1. Your principal has asked you to give a short speech at graduation.

_____
_____
_____

_____ 2. Your mom asks you how your day was.

_____
_____
_____

_____ 3. Your coach asks you to explain why you were late for practice.

_____
_____
_____

_____ 4. You want to let your dad know how much you appreciate him.

_____
_____
_____

_____ 5. Your summer camp counselor asks you to teach some younger campers how to tie slipknots.

_____
_____
_____

~~~~~~

_____ 6. You find out that you are going on the vacation of your dreams!

_____

_____

_____

_____ 7. You get a bad grade on a test for which you studied hard.

_____

_____

_____

_____ 8. You want to wish your best friend a Happy Birthday!

_____

_____

_____

_____ 9. You want to let your brother who is away at college know how you feel about him.

_____

_____

_____

_____ 10. You need to express your sadness because your pet has died.

_____

_____

_____

_____ 11. You decide to enter a contest to win a gift certificate to your favorite store. All you have to do is create a way to motivate people to shop there.

_____

_____

_____

Contract

I've got an offer you can't refuse!

If I do these things: _____

_____

_____

On this timeline: _____

Then I get to: _____

_____

Student _____

Teacher _____

Date _____

3 Listening and Speaking

Hearing is one of the most powerful senses by which we receive information and acquire knowledge. Adequate hearing is essential for the normal development of speech and language, but normal hearing does not guarantee adequate listening skills. Many people with normal hearing do not have adequate auditory processing skills. That is, individuals can hear sounds in the environment and understand others' speech, but they do not have the listening skills to attend, discriminate, remember, sequence, analyze, or synthesize sounds and words.

Students with learning disabilities frequently have deficits in the auditory channel of communication. They do not process auditory information very well, and as a result, they do not easily learn by listening. Young children with auditory processing deficits have difficulty rhyming words, learning phonics, and writing letters by listening to "the sound the letter makes." These children frequently substitute words that sound similar. For example, a student sold some candy for his school. Because he sold all of the candy, he thought he should receive a *commitment*. What he meant to say was, *commission*. These two words sound similar, they have the same number of syllables; however, they have very different meanings. Teachers of older students with listening deficits commonly cite spelling and listening comprehension as areas of particular difficulty. Teenagers and adults with auditory processing deficits frequently misunderstand puns, jokes, and innuendoes. Individuals who have normal hearing but do not adequately process information presented through the auditory channel are often diagnosed as having central auditory processing deficits (CAPD). These individuals learn more easily and quickly when information is presented in multisensory ways.

A young child with CAPD might exclaim, "He's a great *sucker* player!" when he actually means, "He's a great *soccer* player!" *Soccer* and *sucker* sound similar to someone with CAPD. You'll notice that the context in which the word was used (*sucker player* vs. *soccer player*) didn't help this person recognize the difference between the two words.

Speech is the ability to correctly form and produce the sounds in a given language. Some speech sounds are formed when both lips come together and the exhaled breath stream is stopped. These sounds are known as bilabial stops (/p, b/). Other sounds are formed when the air stream is interrupted, and the tongue tip touches the hard palate right behind the upper front teeth. The /t/ sound is an example. Some sounds are voiced and others are voiceless. The vocal cords vibrate for the voiced sounds (all vowel sounds, /m, z, l/), but not for the voiceless sounds (/p, s, f/). A large percentage of children with learning disabilities have speech delays and speech disorders.

Language is generally described as having three major components:
- *Form* (phonology, morphology, and syntax)
- *Content* (semantics)
- *Use* (pragmatics)

Specific rules apply to form, and individuals learn to combine sounds and words according to these rules. Semantics, or word meaning, can be determined from single words (*building*), but meaning often only becomes clear when words are placed in context (He is *building* a *building*.). Pragmatics combines form and content into functional and socially appropriate communication. Individuals who have difficulty with pragmatics may have trouble fitting in with their peers because they say inappropriate things or behave in ways others might describe as "weird." They can't read the listener's cues to end a conversation naturally, or they switch the topic of conversation without signaling a change. A learning disability is a language disorder; that is, a person with a learning disability has difficulty sending or receiving the symbols in spoken or written language.

This chapter provides multisensory activities that will enhance auditory processing skills, improve speech production, and improve expressive and receptive language. Many of the activities will incorporate listening and speaking because these skills are highly dependent on one another. You'll notice that some activities are similar to ones in other chapters, yet their focus is different.

Goals

- To enhance auditory processing skills
- To promote correct speech production
- To model standard oral English
- To increase receptive and expressive language skills
- To heighten awareness about nonverbal language
- To develop an understanding and respect for speakers from different linguistic and dialectical backgrounds

| L1 | **Magnetic Letters and Sounds** | Standard: 3 |

Words are made up of individual sounds. Many students have difficulty analyzing words into their component sounds. Magnetic letters help students "see the sounds" because the letters help the students understand the number and positioning of single sounds or groups of sounds within a word (s-a-p; tr-i-p).

Place magnetic letters (some consonants and vowels) on a magnetic board in front of each student. Say a word one sound at a time. The student selects the individual letter sounds and builds the word working from left to right on the magnetic board. Have the student orally read the completed word.

| L2 | **Blending** | Standards: 3, 6 |

Blending sounds can be improved upon by using the magnetic board and letters described in activity **L1**. Begin by placing individual letters that form a word in order on a magnetic board. Then space the letters apart on the board. Have the student say the sound each letter makes as he slowly moves them closer together. The student continues to say each sound and to move the letters closer together until there is no space between the letters. The word should become apparent as the space between the letters diminishes, and the sounds are spoken more closely together. Students can write each word after they have blended the sounds orally, and then they can read the word aloud.

| L3 | **Word Building** | Standards: 3, 6 |

Index cards with individual sounds, categories of sounds (blends, vowel digraphs), types of syllables (open, closed, VCE), or prefixes and suffixes can be used to build words. Students work in pairs to build words using the index cards. Have one student dictate each word to another student as the word is made. The recorder writes it in a word list. Each pair of students reads its word list. The teams compare how many different words were built from the same set of index cards. Here's an example of how several words can be made from a few index cards:

| de | miss | tail | tour | ed |

Word List

detail	detour	tailed
detailed	detoured	toured
	missed	

| L4 | **Hit the Target** | Standards: 3, 6 |

Words from word families lend themselves to rhyme. Write words within word families on index cards. Highlight the word family in each word by writing the family letters in colored pen or with larger, bolder letters (**fat**, **cat**). You can also use colored index cards to emphasize different word families. Randomly place the words on the classroom or gym floor. Have a student toss a beanbag onto a card and supply a word that rhymes with it. For example, here are some words you might use from the **-in** family:

| sp**in** | gr**in** | t**in** | ch**in** | f**in** |

Here are some different types of cards you can make for this beanbag toss game:
- Words with similar affixes
- Words that use similar spelling or grammar rules
- Matching words with their definitions
- Cloze sentences with specific vocabulary

Another variation is to write pairs of rhyming words and non-rhyming words on cards and place them on the floor. Have one student toss a beanbag onto a card. The student reads the two words aloud, and another student listens and determines if the pair of words rhymes. Here are a few card examples:

| load / lead | melt / felt | deer / dare |

| L5 | **Concentration** | Standards: 3, 6 |

Auditory and visual cues can increase listening and memory skills. Find pairs of words that have the same linguistic components, such as the following:
- comparative and superlative adjectives (*larger/heavier, largest/heaviest*)
- verb tense (*bumped/hopped*)
- words with short vowel sounds vs. words with long vowel sounds (*hat/hate*)

Write the words on the same colored index card or paper, or write the words in the same colored marker. Place the pairs of words facedown on a table or desk. Two students take turns turning over one of the colored cards and reading the word aloud, and then turning over another card of the same color and reading that word aloud. His partner has to determine how the words match (sound the same; have the same suffix, prefix, or meaning; or are semantically similar). If the student correctly identifies a match, the cards are removed from the group. If the student incorrectly identifies the match, the cards are turned over and the student tries to find a matching pair.

L6	**Match It!**	Standards: 3, 6

Color is a visual cue that helps students attend to targeted components of words, phrases, or sentences (sounds, base words, affixes, irregular spellings). Color-coded words highlight important aspects within each word (pluralization, verb tense).

Students can play "Match It!" with color-coded targeted words. Begin by writing target words on index cards and highlight key components within the words with color. For example, if you are working on adverbs, you might make cards like these, calling attention to the *-ly* suffix with a colored highlighter or writing the suffix in different-colored ink:

quickly		safely

Hold up a card and call on a student to say a word that matches the target word in some way. You might have the student provide a word that means the same, has the opposite meaning, or contains the same suffix. If you wish to make this a class activity, have students write their individual responses on dry erase boards. Have all the students hold their answers up at once so you can check them immediately.

L7	**Say It, Circle It, Write It**	Standards: 3, 6

Sound-symbol associations are emphasized when students say a word, then they circle the word, and then they write the word. You can find a sample of this kind of activity to use with your students on page 38. You can easily create similar worksheets for your students using computer clip art and vocabulary or spelling words from content subjects.

L8	**Cloze with Rhyming Words**	Standards: 3, 6

Rhyming is one of the earliest developing phonological awareness skills. Many children with learning disabilities have difficulty recognizing the sound pattern in words. They don't recognize pairs of rhyming words, nor can they supply a rhyming word for one provided by the teacher. Context can aid the students' rhyming skills and develop their vocabulary and expressive language.

Write the following rhyming patterns on laminated index cards. One student reads the phrase to another student who writes an appropriate rhyming word on the index card using a grease pen or erasable marker.

You take a *pill* when you are _____   Jack and *Jill* went up the _____

Shake and _____   *Bake* a _____

The *cat* in the _____   *Shop* till you _____

Beat the _____   Snug as a *bug* in a _____

| L9 | **Topic Poems** | Standards: 2, 3, 4, 5, 6, 7, 8, 9, 10, 11, 12 |

Vocabulary, categorization, and memory skills are required for poems. You can provide students with examples of a wide range of poems from different periods to build an understanding of different writing styles and uses of language. Students can research different poets to learn about a poet's life and body of work.

Give students a topic, and have them tell you words related to the topic. Write the words on the board or on an overhead projector for the class to view. Encourage students to use a print or electronic thesaurus to expand the word list. Ask students from different cultural backgrounds to provide appropriate "home words" or slang to the word list. Students who are bilingual can provide vocabulary in their native language and its English equivalent. Here's an example:

Topic
violence

Student Word List

senseless	anger	hurt
mean	enemies	danger

Have each student select words from the topic list to write a poem, or have the class work collaboratively to write a poem. Publish the final poems in the school newspaper, and encourage students to draw pictures to accompany their poems.

| L10 | **List, Blend, and Spell** | Standard: 3 |

Letters have names (**m** = *em*, and **s** = *es*) and letters "say" sounds (**m** says "mmm" and **s** says "sss"). Blending sounds is an important reading decoding skill, and it is essential for spelling accuracy. Identifying and blending sounds in words are sound-symbol awareness activities. Writing the sounds in words strengthens a student's memory for the sound-symbol association, sound categories (blends and vowel diagraphs) and phonetic spelling rules.

The **List, Blend, and Spell** activity on page 39 requires sound analysis, sound blending, and spelling skills. Record the student's accuracy for saying, blending, and listing the sounds in the words, as well as for spelling accuracy. Use your students' weekly spelling or vocabulary words for this activity.

| L11 | **It's In the Bag** | Standards: 4, 10, 11 |

Expressive language activities require students to use descriptive vocabulary, and the activities improve students' vocabulary, content knowledge, and speech production. The following expressive language activity requires students to use their tactile sense to describe objects.

Collect items that reflect content vocabulary, such as a test tube, test tube brush, beaker, and test tube stopper. Place one item in a cloth or paper bag. Have one student reach into the bag, select an item, and hold it inside the bag without looking into the bag. Have the student describe the item (without saying its name) while the other students guess the name of the item that is being described.

Several variations on this activity can be implemented depending on the age of the student and the target vocabulary. Instead of describing an object, do the following:

- Have a student read the definition of an item in the bag. Have the other students name the item.
- Write vocabulary words on note cards and put them in a bag. Have a student reach into the bag, and pull out one card. The student says a sentence using the vocabulary word.
- Have a student pantomime the function or use of an item while other students try to name the item.
- Write non-English words on cards and place them in a bag. Have a student reach in, pull out a card, and translate the word (French: *chien/dog*)

| L12 | **People Board Games** | Standards: 3, 4, 6, 12 |

Students' attention and motivation for learning may be increased when they engage in learning activities that involve motor activities. Instead of playing traditional tabletop board games with inanimate markers, build a game board path on the floor of the classroom, gym, or playground with chalk or colored tape. You might draw a checkerboard or plot a maze on the floor. Students can either move along the game board as they correctly answer questions, or they can be ousted from the board because of an incorrect answer. You might write instructions for game movement and give them to players as they move along the board (e.g., "Go back one space" or "Trade places with another player"). Students might play in teams and consult with one another before the captain answers the question. Devise games that require strategy, attention, and knowledge in order to win. Content subject matter, vocabulary, spelling, etc., can be used as the basis for game questions.

| L13 | **Voice Control** | Standards: 2, 4, 7, 9, 10, 12 |

Students appreciate language and learn about diverse genres of literature by orally reciting literature. Various forms of literature (poetry, speeches, and editorials) can be researched and selected according to relevant curriculum content or theme. Have students select their own pieces of literature to recite or provide selections for them. Then have students orally present their literature pieces using the pitch, volume, rhythm, and pronunciation that appropriately match the mood and tone of the piece. Students can further set the tone or mood of their selections by dressing in costume to depict the time the piece was written or a character in the text. Students develop critical listening skills by practicing their presentations in front of their peers who will listen and provide constructive feedback regarding their classmates' delivery.

Two online references for titles of appropriate literature with a variety of dialects are American Dialect Society (http://www.american dialect.org/biblio.html) and Dialect Variation in Children's Literature that contains bibliographic information for African-American, Latino, Creole, Cajun, Irish, and other regional dialects (http://www.streetcat.bnkst.edu/html/dialectbib.html).

| L14 | **Language Dominoes** | Standards: 4, 9, 10, 12 |

Write content vocabulary, spelling words, or grammatical phrases on index cards. Have students work together to organize the words and phrases into complete sentences. Encourage different groups of students to form different types of sentences using the same words and phrases. For example, have one group create a declarative sentence and another group create an interrogative sentence using the same group of words. When each group has created its sentence, have a group member read the sentence aloud and ask the rest of the class to determine which type of sentence each group is saying. Help students understand that word order and vocal inflection are required for others to realize the differences between declarative, interrogative, and imperative sentences. For example, the same sentence can be read in different ways to depict different types of sentences:

- I'm going to the store. (*declarative*)
- I'm going to the store? (*interrogative*)
- I'm going to the store! (*imperative*)

This activity will benefit students whose first language is not English. Vocabulary and grammar skills are developed, and students learn how vocal inflection impacts meaning.

| L15 | **Barrier Games** | Standards: 4, 12 |

Barrier games require detailed expressive language and adequate auditory attention and memory skills. Two students play the game. The object of the game is for one student to give another student step-by-step directions for completing a maze, navigating a map, etc. The speaker's oral directions have to be complete and sequential in order for the listener to successfully complete the task. The content of the directions can vary according to the purpose of the activity (ordinal numbers, directionality, terms and definitions).

| L16 | **Choral Reading for Listening Comprehension** | Standards: 1, 2, 3 |

Comprehension and memory for story elements are improved through choral reading. Choose an age-appropriate poem or story segment your students will enjoy reading. Then have the entire class or a small group of students orally read the same passage. Each student must attend to the text in order to keep up with the group, and because the passage is read orally, students' decoding and comprehension skills are enhanced. In addition, students who have decoding difficulties and who are reluctant to read aloud can find relative anonymity in choral reading activities.

| L17 | **Watch What I Say** | Standards: 3, 4, 6, 8, 11 |

The use of videotaped presentations allows students to watch *how* the speaker conveys important information. These visual cues alert the listener to important information about the way speakers communicate. Have a student recite a poem or story segment or tell a personal anecdote while you videotape the presentation.

Play the tape for the class and have students list the visual cues used by the speaker, and then have them discuss why these cues are important. Replay the video so that students can verify their list of cues and identify other cues they might have missed during the first viewing. You might have students view video recordings of yourself modeling proper visual cues. Have students write the visual cues and their meanings as they occur. Lead a class discussion about the different types and meanings of the cues.

Here are some visual cues to address in this activity:
- Gestures
- Facial expressions
- Movement away or toward the audience
- Use of props (laser pointers, sample products)
- Use of graphics (tables, charts, models)

35

| L18 | **Performance Vocabulary** | Standards: 1, 7, 9, 12 |

Listening and vocabulary skills can be advanced through music. Music brings new ideas, interests, and vocabulary into the classroom. Collaborate with your school's music teacher to build language themes around music. Play pieces of music that coincide with classroom content, such as a historical period or particular theme, and discuss how the piece of music relates to the content area. Also have students research information to learn about various types of music and the lives and home countries of different composers. Students can be introduced to music from different countries to deepen their understanding of and respect for diversity in cultures, ethnic groups, and geographic regions.

Here are a few vocabulary terms and a music glossary website (*A-Z Glossary of Music* http://www.hnh.com/mgloss.htm) you may find helpful when introducing and discussing musical performances:

lyrics	aria	opera	metronome
octave	chorus	ensemble	scale
Gregorian chant	interlude	percussion	movement
section	measure	Philharmonic	bravado

| L19 | **Get Your Newspaper** | Standards: 1, 3, 4, 5, 6, 11, 12 |

You can use a stack of old newspapers to generate discussion and written language. Find an interesting photograph of a news event from a recent newspaper and cut it out. Make sure you select a picture that really tells a story. Cut off the caption of the photograph and make several photocopies of it. (Note: Photocopying newspaper pictures often results in variable quality. Another option is to collect several copies of the same newspaper edition, cut out the same picture in the copies, and remove the caption.) Give a photograph to each small group of students. Encourage the groups to discuss the content of the photograph, the emotion the photograph evokes, etc. Have each group write a caption of its own for the photograph. You might have students draw additional pictures to accompany the original photograph. Their drawings can depict what might have occurred prior to or following the photograph, what might have occurred if one of the people in the photograph hadn't been there, etc.

When the groups have finished, have them compare their captions and drawings for similarities and differences. Then have the class vote to decide which groups' caption or drawing best describes the photograph. Display the winning team's photograph, picture, and caption in the classroom.

References

Felzer, L. (n.d.). A multisensory reading program that works. Retrieved August 1999, from http://www.csupomona.edu/~ljfelzer/read.htm

Galletly, S. (1999). *Sounds & vowels: keys to literacy progress.* Mackay Q, Australia: Literacy Plus, Mackay.

Harvey, D. (n.d.). Teaching ESL with music. Retrieved July 30, 2001, from http://www.teachnet.com/lesson/langarts/esl/techingeslwithmusic.html

I'm dreaming of a rhyme christmas. (n.d.). Retrieved July 30, 2001, http://www.teachnet.com/lesson/langarts/writing/rhymechristmas.html

Spector, C. C. (1999). *Sound effects: activities for developing phonological awareness.* Eau Claire, WI: Thinking Publications.

Say It, Circle It, Write It

Name _____

Say the name of the two pictures. Listen to the sounds in the beginning, middle, and end of each word. Circle the word that completes the sentence. Then write the circled word on the line.

1.

   spy   sky

   The _____ is a very calm shade of blue.   _____

2.

   fifty   twenty

   _____ cents is twice as much as two nickels.   _____

3.

   penny   pony

   A brown _____ is a faithful friend.   _____

4.

   hurdling   cheering

   _____ is a difficult track skill.   _____

List, Blend, and Spell

Name _____

Put a check (✔) over each individual sound unit as you say it. Then say the word. Finally, write the word on the blank.

1. sh – ir – t   _____

2. b – ar – n   _____

3. l – oo – k   _____

4. spl – a – sh   _____

5. ch – ur – ch   _____

6. cr – a – ck   _____

7. tr – ai – n   _____

8. fl – oa – t   _____

9. r – u – sh – ed   _____

10. gr – ou – n – d   _____

11. kn – o – ck   _____

12. b – ea – r   _____

13. f – ai – n – t   _____

14. w – i – th   _____

15. re – fl – e – x   _____

Variation: Have the class, in unison, complete the activity. Have students say each sound unit, say the word, and orally spell the words instead of writing the words.

4 Reading

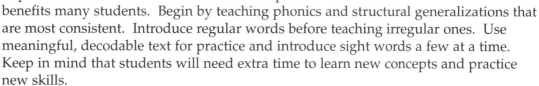

Students with learning disabilities often need structured, systematic, and cumulative reading instruction. Because these students do not grasp new concepts intuitively, your instruction should be direct and explicit. Content should include phonology and phonological awareness, syllabication/morphology, syntax, and semantics (Schupack & Wilson, 1997).

Instruction that begins with whole to part, moves to part to whole, and then back to whole to part benefits many students. Begin by teaching phonics and structural generalizations that are most consistent. Introduce regular words before teaching irregular ones. Use meaningful, decodable text for practice and introduce sight words a few at a time. Keep in mind that students will need extra time to learn new concepts and practice new skills.

Although many of the activities in this chapter are presented in isolation, they should be combined with real reading and writing in order to make learning meaningful. For example, when learning specific letter sounds, students should learn words that contain those sounds and listen to or read stories that contain words with the target sounds. When learning new vocabulary words and their definitions, students should experience the words in literature and use them in their own writing.

To help students progress, read aloud to them so that they develop a love for literature and experience rich vocabulary and ideas beyond their own reading levels. Surround them with high-quality, interesting books as well as functional reading materials, such as telephone books, computer manuals, menus, and newspaper ads.

Goals

- To decode text
- To learn new vocabulary
- To understand text and language and how to use them
- To apply many strategies to comprehend text
- To understand connections between written and spoken language
- To enjoy different genres of literature and other text
- To read fluently for many purposes
- To understand and respect diversity
- To share literacy experiences with others

| R1 | **Skywriting** | Standard: 3 |

Many students benefit from skywriting. To skywrite, students use two fingers to write letters and new words in the air as they look at the print and say the word. (Using two fingers forces them to use more of the entire arm for movement, which involves large muscles.) Skywriting is very practical because it requires no preparation or materials and can be used in many content areas.

| R2 | **Textured Surfaces** | Standard: 3 |

Students can use textured surfaces to trace new letters and/or vocabulary words with two fingers as they say or spell them. Sandpaper or carpet squares make great textured surfaces for tracing. Many students like to write in sand trays, which consist of a thin layer of sand spread on a flat baking sheet. Others like to place writing paper over sand paper and write on the writing paper with crayon. Some are motivated by tracing letters and words with their fingers on thick plastic bags filled with finger paint. (Do not fill the bags too full, and make sure they are sealed well. You may even want to double the bags.) If older students are embarrassed to use these surfaces, they can trace words on the legs of their blue jeans or a desk surface.

Using textured surfaces to make learning multisensory need not be limited to reading class. Textured surfaces can be used as students recite math facts, state capitols, and scientific formulas. The possibilities are endless!

| R3 | **Letter Manipulatives** | Standard: 3 |

Students can move letter manipulatives as they look at and say letters and words. Possible manipulatives include the following:

✔ Magnetic letters on cookie sheets (Draw or tape lines on the cookie sheet to help with letter placement and spacing.)

✔ Felt letters on flannel boards or individual sheets of flannel (Glue lines on the flannel to aid placement and spacing.)

✔ Sponge letters soaked in paint to print on art paper

✔ Plastic letters to arrange on a table top

✔ Sandpaper letters pasted on cards (Draw a heavy line on the card to indicate letter placement on lines. Color code these by putting uppercase letters on one note card color and lowercase letters on another.)

✔ Sandpaper letters pasted on empty paper towel rolls (Stand these upright.)

✔ Student-made clay letters (Add a drop of scent to the clay to add additional sensory stimulation.)

✔ Student-made pipe cleaner letters

| R4 | **Picture Sorts** | Standards: 3, 6, 10 |

Picture sorts can be used for students to practice many different letter-sound relationships (initial, medial, final sounds; short and long vowels; digraphs; diphthongs; spelling patterns). For example, here are the steps for picture sorting according to initial consonant blends:

1. Write the names of two or more consonant blends on separate cards. Place the cards at the top of the desk in a horizontal line.

2. Provide cards with recognizable pictures of words that start with those consonant blends.

3. As students pronounce the word for each picture, have them exaggerate the initial blend and place the picture card in the correct column.

4. Have students make additional picture cards by drawing or cutting and pasting, and take turns sorting each other's pictures.

5. Have students write the correct initial consonant blend on the back of each picture card for self-correction.

6. If you have bilingual students, let them make picture cards for words of their own language and share them with other students.

| R5 | **Raised Letters** | Standard: 3 |

Raised lettering allows students to touch and trace words as they sound them out or spell them aloud. Write words with puffy paint or thick glue (tinted with food coloring). Other materials, such as rice or sand, can be glued to letters to make a rough surface for tracing. Students with legible handwriting can make their own cards for new vocabulary words. Students who write very slowly or illegibly will need help.

| R6 | **Personalized Letter Cards** | Standard: 3 |

Many teachers post alphabet letters on cards in their classrooms. You can have students make their own cards by forming a letter on a card using a material that starts with the letter's sound. For example, use a pipe cleaner to form **P** and candy pieces for hard **C**. Other ideas for materials to form letters are yarn for **Y**, buttons for **B**, seeds for **S**, rope for **R**, gold paper for **G**, velvet for **V**, noodles for **N**, lace for **L**, and tissue for **T**. Have your students brainstorm ideas for materials to use for the other letters.

| R7 | **Letters in Names** | Standards: 3, 6, 11 |

Using classmates' names as key words to remember letters and their sounds is personal and motivating to many students. When students study particular letters, let them find the letter and its sound(s) in the names of classmates. You can even have them make a bulletin board with classmates' photographs. Write the names by the photos and highlight the focal letter. An extension of this activity is to also write a one-word piece of information about each classmate with the focal letter highlighted. Examples include the states and countries that students were born in, the streets they live on, the months of their birthdays, or their favorite foods.

A̲my

L̲ake L̲ane

Louisi̲an̲a

U.S.A̲.

A̲pril

A̲pple

| R8 | **Letter Folders** | Standards: 3, 6 |

Draw a dark line on the inside of a file folder at the very top. Under it, place sticky notes in horizontal lines. On each sticky note, write one letter of the alphabet. Provide one of these folders for each student.

Make a list of vocabulary words that students need to be able to spell. Call out each word, one at a time. As you call each word, ask students to move the letters on the sticky notes to spell the new word on the dark line. Before moving on to the next word, have a student say and spell the new word on the board or overhead to check accuracy. Ask a student volunteer to provide a meaningful sentence that contains the word.

| R9 | **Letter Cut-Ups** | Standards: 3, 6 |

Letter Cut-Ups can help students read and spell new words. Begin by writing the new word on two strips of paper. Have students cut one of the words apart into its individual letters. Then mix up the cut-apart letters and let students move the letters to spell the word correctly using the complete word as a model. If it is a phonetically regular word, students can sound the word out phoneme-by-phoneme as they move letters. If it is a sight word, help them notice things about the word that will help them remember it. For example, the word *friend* has *end* on the end.

44

R10	I Spy	Standards: 3, 6

"I Spy" is an excellent game that teaches students to use oral language to describe familiar objects. A variation of traditional "I Spy" is to ask students to start off by naming the letter that occurs at the beginning of the object they spy. As students become more astute with decoding skills, they might name other features of the word, too. For example, a student might say, "I spy something that starts with **K**. It is a compound word. It is used to put information into a computer." (*keyboard*)

R11	Pocket Charts	Standards: 3, 6, 10

Pocket charts and card squares or sentence strips can be used in many ways to provide multisensory instruction. Here are just a few examples:

- Students can manipulate individual letters written on card squares and put them in a pocket chart as they sound them out. (Be sure they pronounce the completed word when they finish.)
- Students can arrange words and punctuation marks on card squares into complete sentences. (Have students read each word as they work and the completed sentence when they finish.)
- Students can put sentences written on sentence strips into sequential order. (Have students read each sentence as they work and all of the sentences in order when they finish.)
- Ask students whose first language is not English to arrange words into sentences in their native languages and translate into written English underneath.

R12	Paper Plate Match-Ups	Standards: 3, 6

Paper plates and clothespins are all you need to make various matching activities. For example, if students are studying prefixes and root words, do the following:

- Draw lines on a paper plate to divide it into pie-shaped wedges. Write a prefix that students are studying on each wedge.
- Write root words that can be used with the prefixes to make new words on clothespins.
- Have students pin the clothespins to the appropriate prefixes. Ask students to list all the words that they make and say a sentence with each one.
- After students have participated in this activity, assign new prefixes to them, and have them make their own paper plate match-ups to share with each other.

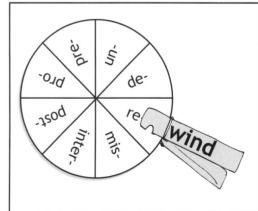

| R13 | **Bean Bag Toss** | Standards: 3, 6 |

Use beanbags to help students practice many different reading skills. For example, if students are studying digraphs, do the following:

1. Using chalk on concrete or a marker on butcher paper, draw large squares.
2. Write a digraph that your students are studying (*ch, sh, wh, ph*) in each square.
3. Have students toss the beanbag toward the squares.
4. Depending on which digraph square the beanbag lands in, have the student say that digraph sound and a word that contains it.

| R14 | **Blending Words** | Standards: 3, 6 |

Many students learn individual letter sounds but still have difficulty blending them into new words. You can play a multisensory card game to give students the opportunity to practice this necessary skill. For example, if students are studying the consonant blends *sp, spl, st,* and *str,* write each blend on a red card. On blue cards, write word endings that can be combined with these blends to make words. (To include more senses, go over the letters with glue, so students can trace the raised blends and endings.)

Have individual students or groups of students manipulate the cards to make as many words as possible. Make sure that they pronounce the sounds on the cards and the finished words as they do the activity. They should also keep a record of words made. When students have finished blending all possible words using the cards, encourage them to think of new words and make blend and ending cards for those. In this way, the number of cards increases, and the game becomes increasingly challenging.

| R15 | **Word Families Strips** | Standard: 3, 6 |

Students can study word families using word family strips. Older students can even make the strips themselves. These are the steps:

1. Write the phonogram being studied toward the end of a strip of cardboard.

   At the beginning of the photogram strip, cut two horizontal slits about the height of one letter.
2. Write initial consonants and blends that students know on another strip of cardboard. Make sure that the strip fits between the slits you cut on the first piece of cardboard.
3. Lace the strip with the initial consonants and blends through the phonogram strip.
4. As students pull each consonant and blend through the phonogram strip, have them pronounce the new word and tell if it is a real word or a nonsense word.
5. If it is a real word, have students make a sentence with it.

| R16 | **Silent Letters** | Standards: 3, 6 |

Students often try to pronounce every letter in words, even though some letters are not heard. To remind students that some letters are silent, give them a list of familiar words. Have students pronounce each word and scribble over or cross out the letters that they do not hear with a dark crayon, as in the example below.

dumb   sign   light   make   stroke   cure

| R17 | **Multisensory Syllabication** | Standards: 3, 6 |

Many students have difficulty hearing individual sounds within words. It is especially important for these students to be able to divide words into syllables or word chunks. To help them do this, write new words on the board. Have students look at the words and pronounce them. As they pronounce, have them do a multisensory action to denote each syllable. For example, as students pronounce each word, they can do the following:

- Clap each syllable
- Hop for each syllable
- Snap their fingers for each syllable
- Bounce a ball for each syllable
- Feel their chin drop on each syllable
- Tap on their desk for each syllable

| R18 | **Multisensory Cue Systems** | Standards: 3, 6 |

All students need to be taught to decode in a flexible manner using the three common cue systems:

1. letter/sound cues (*graphophonics*)
2. structure cues (*word order and parts of speech in sentences, syntax*)
3. meaning cues (*semantics*)

You can analyze students' uses of the cue systems to decode unfamiliar words as they read orally. Observe behavior clues such as these:

- Do they sound words out? (*letter/sound cue*)
- Do they reread sentences to figure words out from context? (*meaning cue*)
- Do they look at pictures to figure words out? (*meaning cue*)
- Do they intuitively know the part of speech of the unfamiliar word ? (*structure cue*)
- Do they search for a word that makes sense? (*meaning cue*)

You can also ask questions such as, "How did you get that word?" or "What made you say that?" As you identify students' use of cue systems to read, you can help them build on their strengths and remediate their weaknesses.

More mature students can analyze their own use of these cue systems. The **Cue Systems** chart on page 64 will help them analyze their own cueing. As students read a passage and come to new words, have them write the word in the first column and note the cue systems that they used to decode and the order that they used them. Also, ask them to try to explain why they used the cues as they did. Here is an example of a partially completed chart:

Name: *Jon*				Date: *Sept. 3*
Word	**Letter/Sounds**	**Structure**	**Meaning**	**Why?**
constellation	*1*	*2*	*2*	*I sounded the first part out. Then I knew the rest.*
Jupiter			*1*	*The book said it was the biggest planet. I knew it was Jupiter.*

After students finish reading, have them go back over their charts and identify the cues they used most and least. Guide the students in a discussion about their use of the cues. Help them to see why they used some cues more than others (they tend to use letter/sound cues more when material is unfamiliar; they tend to use meaning cues more when they have good background knowledge). Also, note your students' weaknesses and strengths and suggest ways to improve their decoding skills. Continue to do this periodically with new reading selections.

R19	**Musical Vocabulary**	Standards: 3, 6

Many students have a difficult time learning new vocabulary words and definitions. Frequently, music will help these students learn. For this activity, students need a music maker of some type. It can be a real instrument (harmonica, keyboard, guitar) or student-made (a shoebox with a thin rubber band stretched over one end and a thick rubber band stretched over the other end).

Have students write a word with a pencil. Then have them trace over the vowels with crayon or marker. Next have students choose two notes on the musical instrument. One note will represent the vowels, and the other note will represent the consonants. As students spell vocabulary words, have them play the appropriate note for each letter. After doing this several times, ask students to give the definition of the word and use it in a meaningful sentence.

R20	**Drawing New Words**	Standard: 3

Have students write each new vocabulary word on one side of a card and outline the shape of the word with a colored marker. On the other side of the card, have them draw a picture that depicts the meaning. Students who do not like to draw can cut a picture from a magazine to paste on the card. As they study the word, encourage them to continue to trace the outline to visually remember short or tall letters, letters that extend below the line, rectangular words, and other word features.

elephant   fossil   grandmother   what

R21	**Word of the Day**	Standards: 3, 6, 7

Have students do daily, in-depth, multisensory study of a new, interesting vocabulary word. Start by putting the heading, *Word of the Day*, on a bulletin board. Then put the headings *Part of Speech, Definition, Antonym, Synonym,* and *Sentence.* Each day, choose a relevant word that students will be motivated to learn, and write the word in colored chalk on the chalkboard. Then do the following:

1. Have students pronounce the word as they clap the syllables.
2. Have them finger-write it on their desktops as they spell it.
3. Ask them how to divide the word into syllables and mark the vowel letter sounds. Let a volunteer come up to the board to do this as everyone says the word.

4. Discuss the word's definition(s) and part(s) of speech.
5. Let students take turns using the word in meaningful sentences. Write some of these sentences on the board.

> *Word of the Day:* **select**
>
> | *Part of Speech:* **verb** | *Definition:* **to choose** |
> |---|---|
> | *Synonym:* **pick** | *Antonym:* **reject** |
>
> *Sentence:* **I used my mouse to <u>select</u> the text.**

6. If the word has antonyms or synonyms, have students provide them. Erase the vocabulary words from the student-provided sentences you wrote on the board, and have a student replace them with the antonyms and synonyms they named. Ask, "Is the meaning the same? Did it change? How?"
7. Each day, assign a different group of students to use creative materials to write the part of speech, definition, antonym, synonym, and a sentence on cards to pin in the appropriate place on the bulletin board.
8. Challenge all students to use the word in daily life. Keep a chart with students' names and add a tally mark when you hear students using the word. When students have a specified number of tally marks, give a small reward.

Variation: Have advanced students research word origins and report their findings to the class.

R22	## Making Words	Standards: 3, 6

Give each student a set of letters that can eventually be combined into one long word. For example, the letters, *p-l-a-n-t-s*, can make up many smaller words (*an, tan, ant, slant, at, sat, pat*) before they are combined to make the word, *plants*. Make sure that the vowels are a different color from the consonants. Have students start by manipulating the letters to make one-letter words, then two-letter words, then three-letter words, and so forth until they combine all of the letters to make the last word.

Write the words that the students make on the board as they call them out. After all the words have been made, help students sort the words according to their spelling patterns. Discuss how changing even one letter can make a new word.

To save time, give older students strips of letters that they can cut apart themselves. Laminate the letters before they are cut to make them last longer. Each time you do this activity, save the bag of letters with a key for the corresponding words. Over time, you will build up quite a collection of words for your class to make (Cunningham & Hall, 1994).

R23	## Vocabulary Search	Standards: 1, 2, 3, 6, 9, 10, 11

Begin by writing your students' vocabulary words on large cards of different colors and posting them in your classroom. Have students trace the letters of the words on their desks as they spell them and clap the syllables as they say them. Then ask students to take turns defining each word and using it in a sentence.

Divide students into teams. Assign a different story or poem that contains many of the vocabulary words to each team. (The story or poem does not have to contain all of the words.) Have members of the team take turns reading their assigned pieces aloud. Encourage other team members to identify the vocabulary words as they are read. Have students write the sentences where they found the words on strips of paper, but instruct them to put a blank line in place of the vocabulary word. After everyone has finished reading, ask each team to show and read their sentences aloud (saying "blank" in the space where the vocabulary should be). The other teams must identify the word that correctly fills the blank.

This activity is more interesting if you use different genres of literature and sprinkle in some words from different cultures and dialects. Bilingual students will enjoy reading literature that contains vocabulary words derived from their first languages. Discuss similarities and differences between these unique vocabulary words and more common ones. Encourage students to use the new words in their own oral and written language.

| R24 | **Sight Word Scavenger Hunt** | Standards: 1, 3, 11 |

Sight words are words that students need to recognize immediately without having to use word attack skills such as sounding out, syllabication, or the dictionary. As you teach students new sight words, ask them to keep a list of the words on a special sight word pad or card. Then ask students to look for these words in their everyday environments (at school, at home, in the car). When possible, ask them to highlight the word and bring the paper that contains the word to class. If it isn't possible to bring the context to class, have them jot the word down with a reminder of where they saw it. Make sure you write the word on the board as students share so they can see and say the words as well as listen to them. Keep a running list of the words they find the most and the least often.

| R25 | **Classroom Labels** | Standards: 3, 10 |

At the beginning of the year, label ten common objects in your classroom, such as *desk, chair, chalkboard, computer, disk,* and *globe*). Go over the labels with students daily. As students begin to memorize the sight words, remove the labels and let the students put them back in the correct locations. When students master your first set of sight words, put up another set. Encourage bilingual students to label the common objects with their native language equivalents. By the end of the year, your room will be covered with sight words that your students know and use.

| R26 | **Personal Word Banks** | Standards: 3, 4 |

Give each student a card file box and note cards. Provide tabs so students can put the letters of the alphabet on blank cards for dividers. As students learn new words, have them write them on one side of a small note card. Let them go over the letters with glue or puffy paint for texture. On the other side, ask them to write the word's definition or a synonym. On a regular basis, have students trace and say their words, provide definitions for them, and use them in sentences. Encourage students to use their alphabetized word banks for real-life reading and writing activities.

| R27 | **Word Sorts** | Standards: 3, 9, 11 |

Students can play word sort games with the cards in their word banks (See **R26** above). Keeping the specific words in students' word banks in mind, call out categories such as the following and have students find words that match:
- Parts of speech
- Subject area (math, science, history)
- Recreational activities
- Technology
- The world

Students can work together in teams and "pool their cards" to provide words that fit the categories you call out. Next they can discuss and agree upon good subcategories that fit their collective words and physically move their cards to sort their words into those subcategories.

For example, if you call out "the world" as a category, one team might look at its words and sort them according to cultures, such as American, Asian, and European, while another team might choose to sort according to landforms, such as mountains, plateaus, and foothills.

After each team finishes, let it present its subcategories to another team. Encourage discussion of the word meanings, categories, and different ways to use the words.

R28	Newspaper and Magazine Search	Standard: 3

Have students search newspapers or magazines for their vocabulary words. Have them highlight the words as they say them. They can also cut out the words to make collages that include other words or items associated with their vocabulary words.

Variations of the activity can include searching for letters or letter sounds, numerals, or math or science symbols. The search can become a race to see which student can find the most items in a pre-set time limit.

R29	Magnetic Parts of Speech	Standards: 3, 6

Write the parts of speech that students are studying on slips of paper and glue them on magnetic strips. Cut them apart and place them at the top of a cookie sheet or other magnetic surface to make a chart. Next, write sentences with these parts of speech and glue them to magnetic strips. Have students cut the words apart and classify them by placing each word under its appropriate heading on the chart. Ask students to use the cut-out words to make sentences of their own. This activity can be combined with diagramming of simple sentences, which many students with learning disabilities find to be helpful.

R30	Games	Standards: 1, 2, 3, 6

Games such as "Bingo," "Concentration," and "Go Fish" are naturally multisensory and can be adapted to fit many areas of learning. Here are some examples to get you started:
- Write letters on Bingo cards. Call out letter names or letter sounds as you play "Letter/Sound Bingo."
- Write sight words on playing cards and play "Sight Word Go Fish."

- Write word opposites on note cards and lay them facedown. Have students use the cards to play "Antonym Concentration." Words with similar meanings can be written on note cards to play "Synonym Concentration. "
- Prepare a simple game board that contains the categories *Genres of Literature, Authors, Titles, Characters,* and *Settings* to play "Literature Jeopardy."
- Cut apart words with affixes and have students race to see which team can put the most word puzzles together in a set time limit.
- Write contractions on cards to be matched up with the words they replace.
- Write letters or words on the squares of old checkerboards. Have students play the game just like traditional checkers, but instruct them to name each letter or word when they land on it.
- Write letters or words on dominoes made from heavy construction paper. Students play the game just like traditional dominoes, but they have to name the letters or words that they match.

Going over the letters/words with glue so that students can trace them with their fingers as they say them makes any of these games more multisensory. Have groups of students make similar games for each other to play. Keep the games and their directions in plastic bags for ease of use and storage.

| R31 | **Preposition Obstacle Course** | Standards: 3, 6, 11 |

Recognizing and using the right prepositions in context is very hard for many students with learning disabilities. They often benefit from acting out prepositions that are position words, such as *on, off, under, over, below, above, beside, between, around,* and *through.* Here's how to play "Preposition Obstacle Course":

1. Arrange chairs, desks, and other furniture into an obstacle course so that students can climb, step, jump, and crawl through it.
2. With a dark marker, write each position word on a large card.
3. Hold up each card and have the entire class pronounce the word. Then hold up each card, one at a time, for students to take turns attempting to follow the directions on each card in sequence to progress through the course. For example, a student may go *over* the chair, *under* the table, *between* two bookshelves, and *beside* the chalkboard. (You will have to put the cards in an order that calls for movements that are actually possible. However, students often enjoy trying to make awkward movements!)
4. For a change, arrange an outdoor obstacle course or do the activity using playground equipment.
5. When cooperative groups of students make obstacle courses for each other, they have so much fun that they often do not even realize they are learning!

| R32 | Position File Banks | Standards: 3, 6, 11 |

Another effective multisensory activity to help students learn
position concepts is to make illustrated file banks. Here are
the steps for making Position File Banks:

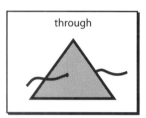

1. Have students pronounce position words you have
   listed on the chalkboard or overhead. Let students take
   turns using items in the room to briefly dramatize each
   word (put a pencil *under* a notebook, put paper *between*
   the pages of a book, wrap tape *around* a paper clip).

2. Provide each student with 10-15 note cards, construction-paper shapes that are approximately one to two
   inches in diameter, and colored string.

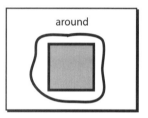

3. Ask students to write a different position word on each
   card and illustrate it using the shapes and colored
   string. For example, they can glue string *beside* a shape,
   between two shapes, *over* a shape).

4. When your students have finished, have them exchange
   cards to orally check the accuracy of their illustrations
   as they trace the position of the string in relationship to
   the shapes.

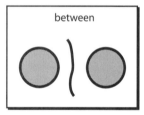

5. Have students file their position word cards in alphabet-
   ical order so they can review position words as they
   read and write.

| R33 | Similes and Metaphors | Standards: 2, 3, 6, 11 |

Figurative language can be very difficult for students to understand, but this activity
can help them with similes and metaphors. Divide students into small groups. Give
each group a piece of fruit, such as a lemon, and have students use their senses to
explore it. Encourage them to look at it, close their eyes and feel it, taste it, toss it lightly
from hand to hand, and so forth. As a class, ask students to list words and phrases that
describe the lemon. They might describe it as firm, sour, tart, bright, and yellow. Then
ask students to make comparisons with other objects with similar characteristics. As
they make the comparisons, model figurative language for them. For example, if students name the sun as something that is similar to a lemon, encourage them to say, "A
lemon is as bright and yellow as the sun" (*simile*) or "A lemon is a bright, yellow sun"
(*metaphor*). Write each simile and metaphor on the board as students say them so they
can see the language patterns. Repeat this exercise with other common objects that can
easily be described with numerous adjectives and adverbs.

As a follow-up, have students make a chart with two columns. Label the first column
Similes and the second column *Metaphors*. As your students read literature from various
genres, have them note similes and metaphors in the correct column. Save these pieces
of figurative language for discussion and creative writing activities.

The LD Teacher's Language Arts Companion:
A Multisensory Approach   54

R34	**Idioms**	Standards: 2, 3, 6, 10

Idioms are another type of figurative language that gives students problems. To help students better understand idioms, call their attention to idioms in literature as they appear. Have students attempt to act out idioms so they can see why the idioms are not to be taken literally. Then have students identify what they think the idioms really mean from the context of the passage. Have them discuss how the idioms make the story more meaningful.

The **Idioms** sheet on page 65 is an example of an activity you can create to give students practice working with idioms they encounter in their readings. (Be sure that students attempt to act out an idiom before identifying its true meaning.) To extend this activity, have students use idioms in their own writing. They can incorporate idioms they read in literature or ones they create themselves. Encourage bilingual students to share idioms from their native languages.

R35	**Teacher Says, "Quotation Marks"**	Standards: 3, 6

Understanding how to use quotation marks in reading and writing is an important task that requires extra effort for many students. This modified version of "Simon Says," called "Teacher Says," will help students master the use of quotation marks.

1. Omitting quotation marks, write sentences that begin with "Teacher says" on sentence strips.
   - Teacher says, Rub your stomach.
   - Teacher says, Touch your nose.
   - Teacher says, Raise your hand.
   - Teacher says, Cross your arms.
   - Teacher says, Run around.

2. Write several sentences that do not begin with "Teacher says" on sentence strips.

3. To play, hold up a sentence strip as you say its direction and place it in a pocket chart. Have students only follow the directions that begin with "Teacher says." Otherwise, they should remain still.

4. After you have used all the sentence strips, ask students how they knew when to follow a direction (when they heard "Teacher says"). Explain that authors use quotation marks to let readers know when people are speaking. Using clothespins with quotation marks on them, illustrate the use of quotation marks by placing the pins in the correct positions on a sentence strip that includes the phrase "Teacher says." Ask students how you knew where to put the quotation marks (around the words that Teacher said). Have students take turns placing quotation marks (clothespins) in the appropriate locations in the remaining sentences.

Note: Students can use a pocket chart with sentence strips and clothespins with other punctuation marks (periods, question marks, exclamation points, commas) to practice more punctuation skills.

| R36 | **Reading with Multiple Senses** | Standard: 3 |

As students read fiction and nonfiction texts, encourage them to use multiple senses. Many need to move their lips (subvocalize) and touch the print as they read. When they come to new words, they often benefit from taking a brief moment to trace them on their desktops or skywrite them as they say them aloud. Many students need to track each line with a finger, strip of construction paper, or a window card (a card with a hole the size of a word or length of a line cut from the middle). Some like to put check marks by each line or paragraph as they finish. Others benefit from using colored pens to underline key concepts as they read and then repeat them. Encourage students to think of other ways to make their reading multisensory.

| R37 | **Before, During, and After Reading Strategies** | Standards: 2, 3 |

Good readers have strategies that they use *before*, *during*, and *after* reading to monitor their comprehension and to learn better. You can make the before, during, and after reading process multisensory for your students in this way:

1. Write the headings, *Before, During*, and *After* in different colors on card stock or heavy paper. Write strategies such as the ones shown on the next page on strips of paper or card stock. Glue magnets to the back of each heading and strategy.

2. Place the headings on a large magnetic surface, such as a wipe-off board or cookie sheet. Mix up the strategies.

3. Before reading, have students classify the strategies by placing them under the correct headings. Model examples of the strategies and let students practice.

4. When first introducing the strategies, simply have students refer to the magnetic board as they read to get ideas for strategies to use.

5. After students have had experience with the strategies, provide each student with a small magnetic board, headings, and strategies. Mix up the strategies. As students use a strategy *before*, *during*, or *after* reading, have them place the magnetic strategy strip in the right category.

6. After everyone finishes, discuss all of the strategies used. Write new strategies on magnetic strips for future activities. Ask students if different genres of literature require different strategies.

Before Reading

- Ask myself what I know about the topic.
- Look through the book and note headings and visual aids.
- Predict what I expect to read.
- Look at questions I will have to answer after reading.

During Reading

- Ask myself if I understand what I am reading.
- If I do not understand:
  - ✔ Reread the sentence.
  - ✔ Read a little farther to see if I understand.
  - ✔ Look at the pictures.
  - ✔ Look up a word in the glossary or dictionary.
  - ✔ Ask someone for help.
- Stop after each section to restate what I read in my own words.

After Reading

- Summarize what I read.
- Ask myself if I need to go back to read any parts again.
- See if I can answer questions about what I read.

57

R38	**Multisensory Recall**	Standards: 1, 2, 3

Visual and auditory imagery, as well as movement, can help students comprehend story events, understand characters' emotions and actions, and vicariously experience fiction and nonfiction. For this activity, select a familiar category, such as objects seen on a playground, activities done at the beach, sounds heard outdoors, or songs heard on the radio. Have students brainstorm to quickly list many ideas that fit the category. Write their ideas on the board. Then have them use imagery to try to memorize the list within a time limit. Cover the board and see who can recall all the ideas on the list. Later, when students read stories, have them use multisensory imagery to fully comprehend and remember what they read. For example, do this:

- Ask students to sketch how they imagine important characters look.
- Ask them to hum the music they imagine that goes along with a particular scene.
- Ask them to move their bodies in a rhythm that matches the story tempo.
- Ask them to mimic facial expressions that demonstrate characters' feelings.
- Ask them to draw the climax of the story.
- Ask them to use body language to show how the story makes them feel.
- If the story is set in a culture other than your students' own, ask them to draw a picture or create a song that would fit that culture.

R39	**Multisensory Riddles**	Standards: 1, 2, 3

Multisensory riddles are another way to encourage students to develop their abilities to use imagery. Make up riddles that are rich with sights, sounds, and smells for students to practice multisensory imagery. The **Multisensory Riddles** sheet on page 66 contains examples to get you started.

R40	**Structured Retellings**	Standards: 1, 2, 3, 4

Having students retell a story serves dual purposes. It helps them comprehend the story and allows you to assess their comprehension. Before reading, discuss the characteristics of the story's genre and tell students the elements that they will be asked to include in their retellings. Some important elements to include are setting, characters, problem to be resolved, attempts to resolve the problem, resolution, theme or moral. Also, to aid memory, have manipulatives that students can use to represent each element. For example, a construction-paper house's roof can represent the setting, a stick figure can represent characters, and a question mark can represent the problem. Have students move the manipulatives from one side of their desks to the other as they include each element in their retelling. When they finish, they can observe which manipulatives have not been moved to know what elements were left out. After a retelling, always discuss the story and relate it to students' experiences.

| R41 | **Flannel Board Retellings** | Standards: 1, 2, 3, 4 |

Retelling a story using flannel board characters is effective because the flannel board characters aid students' memories. The words to a story can also be glued to flannel so that students can add the text to their retelling as well. Sometimes, students enjoy looking at the flannel board characters and scenes and writing the text in their own words. They can then glue the sentences they wrote to flannel and use them to retell the story.

| R42 | **Magnetic Retellings** | Standards: 1, 2, 3, 4 |

Letting students retell a story using magnetic pictures and words is highly motivating. In preparation, duplicate a simple story with multiple pictures. Cut the pictures and text apart, separating the text from the pictures. Attach magnetic tape to the back of the pictures and text.

Have the students listen to the story or read it. Next, ask them to retell the story as they place the pictures in sequential order on a magnetic surface. Then have them place the corresponding text under each picture. Students can check their work using a copy of the story.

A variation of this activity occurs when students leave out a picture or two and ask a partner to guess what story event is missing. Beginning readers may look at the storybook to match the magnetic pictures and text rather than trying to work from memory. Students may also write their own stories for use in this activity. Don't forget to discuss and do follow-up activities to make the stories personally meaningful.

| R43 | **Flannel Board Story Maps** | Standards: 2, 3, 6 |

To help students understand literature better, help them make story maps. Have them write the title of the story in a circle in the center of a page. They can then draw lines that radiate from the title to other circles that contain the setting, characters, plot, and resolution. To make this activity multisensory, have students cut the story map circles out and glue felt on the back. Then they can cut out straight lines made of felt to connect the circles. Have students tell their stories as they place the story map pieces on the flannel board.

More advanced students can classify each story map according to a genre of literature, such as fairy tale, fable, science fiction, historical fiction, or mythology. They can add these labels to their flannel board story maps.

| R44 | **Poetry Puzzles** | Standards: 1, 2, 3, 4, 11 |

Students like poetry, especially if it relates to their own lives. To help them read and understand poems, follow these steps to make Poetry Puzzles.

1. Ask students to copy the words to a familiar poem in large letters on one side of a heavy sheet of paper. (If students have difficulty with this, you can write the poem for them.)

2. On the other side, have students illustrate the poem and cut the picture into puzzle pieces.

3. Mix the pieces up and ask students to put the poem back together with the text side up. Students can check their work by sliding the puzzle onto a piece of cardboard and flipping it over to see if the illustration appears correctly. Have the students practice reading the poem with expression and fluency.

4. As a variation, have each student make a puzzle from a different poem. Have students exchange puzzles to work with, read, and discuss. (For repeated use, laminate the puzzles before cutting them apart and place the pieces in plastic bags.)

| R45 | **Touch-Interactive Technology** | Standards: 1, 2, 3, 8 |

Most classes have access to computers either in the classroom or a computer lab. Many commercial publishers produce books on computer software that allow students to interact with the text through touch. For example, some programs allow children to touch words to hear them pronounced, others allow them to touch characters to hear dialog, and others allow them to touch icons to hear sound effects that make literature come alive. These programs provide multisensory instruction, allow extra practice for students who need it, and can be very motivating.

A Word of Caution: Be sure to preview all software before letting students use it. Work a part of the program with students before allowing them to continue alone and monitor them as they work. Be careful not to let computer technology be used solely for entertainment and never as busy work.

| R46 | **Language Experience Approach** | Standards: 1, 2, 3, 4, 5, 6, 9, 10, 11, 12 |

The language experience approach is a multisensory activity through which students are motivated to read stories that they create about their own experiences. They also learn about text and language and are often able to decode/comprehend beyond their usual ability levels. This approach is especially good for students who are just beginning to learn English. On the following page are the steps for a group language experience story; however, the language experience approach can also be used for individuals:

1. Students must have had a common, interesting experience, such as a field trip, classroom visitor, hobby, sporting event, class pet, or science project.

2. Students take turns dictating sentences about the experience to you.

3. On large chart paper, write exactly what the students dictate. Say each word aloud as you write it and ask students questions about punctuation marks they want to use, dialect they want to include, and so forth.

4. After the story is finished, move your hand under the words in a smooth fashion, as the students read the story in unison with you.

5. After reading and listening to the story this first time, have students choose a title and decide if they want to revise the story.

6. Once again, have students practice reading the story in unison as you or a student volunteer smoothly moves a hand or pointer under the words.

7. Students take turns reading their own individual sentences and those of peers until each one can read the entire story independently.

8. Post the story in the room and have students participate in follow-up activities such as reading the story to partners, creating illustrations, copying the story to take it home to share, or binding it to make a class book. You can also use the story to practice reading skills and concepts. You might have students circle the affixes, highlight the consonant blends, put a box around the names of the characters, trace the punctuation marks with puffy paint, etc.

9. As a variation of this approach, let students create original stories of different genres together.

The <u>Cl</u>ass Pet
by
Mr. <u>Dr</u>ew's <u>Cl</u>ass

For several days, our <u>cl</u>ass had a pet <u>sn</u>ake! We named it <u>Sn</u>eaky.

<u>Sn</u>eaky was <u>gr</u>eat fun to <u>pl</u>ay with. That is, he was fun until he escaped! We searched everywhere.

Finally, <u>Bl</u>ake found him in the <u>pl</u>ant. We gave <u>Sn</u>eaky to <u>Gr</u>ace's mom who is a pet <u>st</u>ore owner. <u>Sn</u>eaky really lived up to his name!

(Underline the consonant blends.)

61

| R47 | **Book Reports** | Standards: 1, 2, 3, 4, 6, 7, 9, 11 |

Have your students develop creative, multisensory book reports as they read many different genres of literature. Here are some suggestions:

- Have students dress in character and tell the story from a main or lesser character's perspective. They will be surprised at how diverse the viewpoints of different characters can be.

- In groups, have students act out the story using simple props and student-written dialog. As a variation, have them change one major action in the story and act out the resulting changes in the story line.

- Have students make flannel board settings and characters to tell the story. (They can also glue student-drawn settings and characters to magnets to tell the story on a magnetic surface.)

- Encourage a group of students to make dioramas depicting sequenced scenes from the story. Each group member can be responsible for making a diorama and telling a different part of the story.

- Have the students illustrate the story scenes on a mural and make up a newspaper-type headline that summarizes each scene.

- Have a group of students rewrite and illustrate the story but change the setting or other story element (time, place, social class, dialect, culture). For example, if a story was set in the past, tell it as if it happened today or in the distant future. If a story happened in the U.S., tell it as if it happened in the Orient. If a story happened in a poor neighborhood, tell it as if it happened in a royal household.

- Let musical students create a song and sing the story using instruments.

- Encourage students who like poetry to write and illustrate a poem about the story.

- After researching the author's life, have students dress up like the author and tell (in the author's voice) how the story came to be written.

The LD Teacher's Language Arts Companion:
A Multisensory Approach

62

References

Cunningham, P. & Hall, D. (1994). *Making words: multilevel, hands-on, developmentally appropriate spelling and phonics activities.* Torence, CA: Good Apple.

Schupack, H. & Wilson, B. (1997). *Reading, writing, and spelling: the multisensory structured language approach.* Baltimore: International Dyslexia Association.

Cue Systems

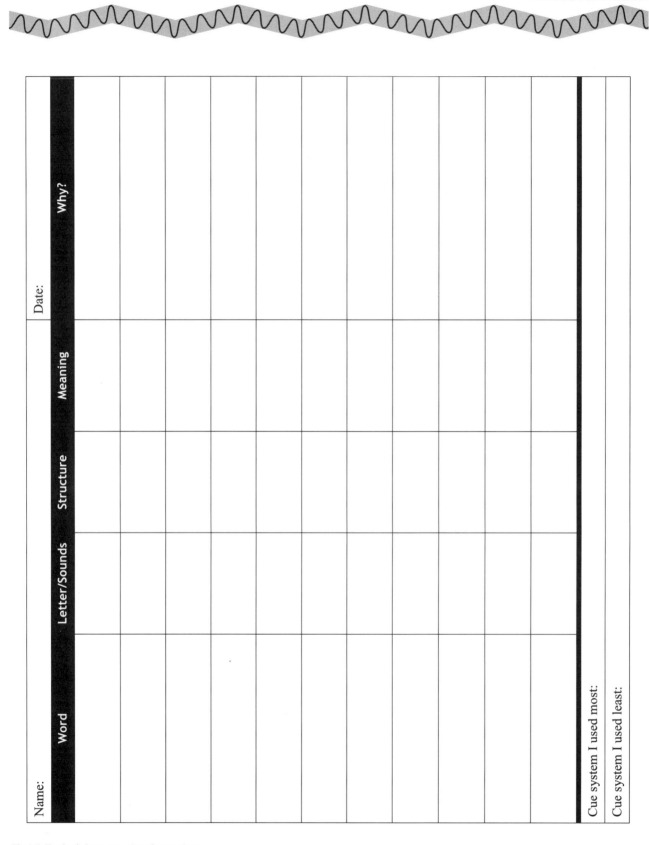

Name: _____ Date: _____

Word	Letter/Sounds	Structure	Meaning	Why?

Cue system I used most: _____

Cue system I used least: _____

Idioms

Name _____

Each sentence below contains an idiom. Read each sentence carefully and visualize what is happening. Try to act out the sentence. Now look at the three choices below the sentence. Mark the one that explains the meaning of the idiom.

1. Judy was a day late and a dollar short for the project.

   ____ a. Judy lacked exactly one dollar needed for the project.

   ____ b. Judy was exactly a day late to begin the project.

   ____ c. Judy was not prepared for the project.

2. Rosie has horses on her brain.

   ____ a. Horses are on top of Rosie's head.

   ____ b. Rosie thinks about horses all of the time.

   ____ c. Rosie's head has been injured by a horse.

3. Whenever someone sells a new product, Carl jumps on the bandwagon.

   ____ a. Carl jumps up on a wagon with a band.

   ____ b. Carl buys the new product quickly without thinking it through.

   ____ c. Carl jumps on a wagon to get away from the salesperson.

4. After winning the contest, Sissy was sitting on top of the world.

   ____ a. Sissy was sitting on top of a high mountain.

   ____ b. Sissy was sitting on a globe after the contest.

   ____ c. Sissy was very happy about winning the contest.

5. Wild horses couldn't keep Raj away from the soccer game.

   ____ a. Raj escaped from the wild horses that were trying to keep him from attending the game.

   ____ b. Nothing could have kept Raj from attending the game.

   ____ c. Raj did not like the wild horses at the soccer game.

Multisensory Riddles

Close your eyes as your teacher or a partner reads these riddles. Imagine the sights, smells, and sounds to help you guess each answer.

1. I am curled up in front of a blazing fire in the fireplace. I have a warm, fuzzy blanket pulled up over my legs. I breathe in the aroma of sweet hot chocolate before taking a sip.

   What kind of weather is outside my window?

2. My friend and I are walking into the dimly lit room and take a seat in chairs that rock when we move. The smell of popcorn fills the air. We hear the rattle of candy being unwrapped. The lights go out as sound and pictures fill the screen at the front of the room.

   Where am I?

3. The noise behind me is loud but cheerful. I can smell gym shoes, textbooks, and lunchboxes. I try hard to concentrate as I turn the stiff steering wheel and carefully guide the long, yellow vehicle into the crowded school parking lot.

   Who am I?

4. I sweat as I play kickball in the hot sun. My new school uniform is scratchy as I kick and run. The bell rings shrilly, and I run to the fountain for a sweet, cool drink of water before class begins.

   Where am I?

5. I stand on the high board and stare at the dark, cool water beneath me. I take a long, deep breath and work up my courage. My heart beats too fast, and I feel a little dizzy. I get a running start and then I dive.

   What am I doing?

5 Written Language

Written language is generally referred to as *writing* — a process that includes much more than the physical act of handwriting letters and numbers onto a piece of paper or typing them on a keyboard to be displayed on a computer screen. Written language is a process that includes the generation of ideas and the transformation of those ideas into organized structures. These structures are recognizable by others and follow accepted rules. Writers, like speakers, monitor what they have written, and they make revisions to clarify information or to correct errors. Once satisfied with the content and form of their writing, writers publish their work for others to read and evaluate. The complexity of the process and the concreteness of the product are two of the most distinguishing features of written language. These distinguishing features may also explain why so many individuals with learning disabilities have significant problems with written language.

Writing is the most complex language process. It is highly governed by rules, but these rules can be arbitrary and inconsistent. Here are just a few examples of the variables that make writing such a complex process:

- Proper nouns begin with an uppercase letter, but common nouns begin with a lowercase letter.
    ✔ *Mrs. Jones, the president, has arrived.*
    ✔ *President Jones has arrived.*

- Different ending punctuation is used with different types of sentences, and the writer uses it to convey meaning.
    ✔ *I'm going.* (Written and read as a declarative, matter-of-fact statement.)
    ✔ *I'm going?* (Written and read as a confused question.)
    ✔ *I'm going!* (Written and read with a strong feeling of frustration.)

- Words that contain short vowel sounds that end in the final /k/ sound are spelled with a **ck** (*smock*); however, words that contain long vowel sounds that end in the final /k/ sound are spelled with a **k-e** (*smoke*).

A writer must learn the rules and correctly apply them in order to meet the standards for written language. Students begin learning these rules as soon as they begin to write their names. A kindergarten teacher probably might say something like this to Paul, a student in her class, as she teaches him to write his name, "Paul, the first letter of your name begins with a 'big' *P*." She helped him understand the difference between the "big *P*" and the "little *p*" by having him trace the two letters on his paper. She pointed out how the "big *P*" touched the top line of his primer writing paper and how the "little *p*" started on the paper's middle dotted line. She used multisensory techniques to highlight the differences between uppercase and lowercase letters, and these techniques helped Paul learn to correctly form and use uppercase and lowercase letters.

This chapter provides multisensory activities for written language. The activities are divided into three categories. First, activities that promote generation of ideas and a plan for writing are presented. Next, specific suggestions to help students learn, remember and apply the structural rules of written language are given. Revising, editing, and publishing activities end the chapter. Even though the chapter is divided into three categories, it is important to remember that writing is a recursive process. That is, as the writer writes, the processes occur simultaneously. Teachers should teach students the entire writing process: all three categories should be developed and encouraged simultaneously.

Goals

- To generate ideas
- To learn visual strategies to organize writing assignments
- To apply knowledge of language structures for written language
  - ✔ Handwriting
  - ✔ Spelling
  - ✔ Sentences
  - ✔ Punctuation
  - ✔ Paragraphs
- To understand and use narrative and expository formats
- To write in a variety of formats for a variety of audiences
- To use technology to support writing
- To engage in the writing process with other writers
- To evaluate written text

68

Generating Ideas and Planning to Write

Depending on the specific requirements of the task, it can take a few minutes or several days to generate ideas and to plan a writing assignment. Students need to learn ways to generate ideas and acquire information on a variety of topics. Provide students with the time and methods to plan for their writing assignments.

W1	**Be a Detective (the 5 Ws)**	Standards: 3, 4, 5, 6, 11

Students need to understand the purpose of the writing assignment before they begin to write. They need to know something about the reader's knowledge of the topic and the requirements of the assignment. Writers are much more likely to successfully complete the assignment if they understand the audience's needs and expectations.

Encourage your students to begin each assignment by examining the 5 Ws questions to help them focus their efforts. The **5 Ws** planning sheet on page 83 will help your students begin the planning process. You can place the **5 Ws** planning sheet on an overhead projector for everyone to see as you go over it together. Provide each student with a copy of the sheet so they can fill in the answers to the questions. Lead the students through the questions and answers. Make blank copies of the **5 Ws** sheet available in the classroom for use with other writing assignments. Modify the questions to meet the needs of the students and the curriculum.

W2	**1-2-3 Get Going**	Standard: 5

The expansiveness of a broad topic can be overwhelming for students with learning disabilities. They frequently have problems generating ideas for a given topic. The process can be less formidable if the topic has a familiar, predictable format.

Begin by having one student describe the steps required to complete a familiar activity or task such as throwing a spiral with a football. The student might provide the following steps:
- First, pick up the football with your throwing hand.
- Second, put your fingertips on the seams.
- Third, pull your arm back.
- Fourth, release the ball as you extend your arm.

You might choose to tape record the steps as the student says them and play the tape back as often as necessary for the student to transcribe the directions. Have other students execute the directions, as transcribed, to determine if the sequence is correct and if all of the steps have been included.

| W3 | **Brainstorming Sessions** | Standards: 3, 4, 5, 6, 9, 11 |

Students can generate ideas about their topic during brainstorming sessions. Ideas, opinions, and information should be freely expressed. Each student can record his own ideas, or one student can be assigned the role of recorder for a group discussion. This is not the time to evaluate the quality of the ideas, so record every idea and suggestion.

| W4 | **Interview** | Standards: 4, 5, 7, 8, 9, 10, 11 |

An interview assignment might reduce a student's anxiety about generating enough information for an assignment. Encourage students to interview fellow students or adults about their interests or a specific topic and write an article about their findings. You can provide a fixed question interview format for students who might have difficulty spontaneously generating specific or appropriate interview questions. Have the student interviewer tape record the interviewee's answers or write them in a notebook as the subject responds to the questions.

Interviews can be a nonthreatening way for students to learn about other cultures and for students who are bilingual to develop their language skills. You can use the opportunity to introduce students to other students or parents who are from different linguistic or cultural backgrounds. Students can research information about the person's country and culture, develop specific interview questions, ask the questions, and write a follow-up article recounting the interview.

| W5 | **Read It, Write It, and Pass It On** | Standards: 3, 4, 5, 6, 10, 12 |

Students with learning disabilities typically write simple sentences. A declarative sentence that contains very few descriptors might be the extent of the sentence's construction. Here's a typical set of simple sentences a student might produce:

I like to ride my skateboard. I like to ride it. It is fun to ride my skateboard.

Groups of students can work together on the "Read It, Write It, and Pass It On" activity. Have a member of the group write one sentence on a given topic and pass the paper to the next student in the group. That student reads the sentence aloud and then writes another related sentence. The paper is passed on to the next person in the group and the process continues around the group until everyone has read aloud and contributed at least one sentence. Here's a typical example:

- **Topic:**   *What do you think is the most popular food in America?*
- **First Sentence:**   *I think pizza is America's most popular food.*
- **First Add-on:**   *Why do you think pizza is so popular?*
- **Second Add-on:**   *Pizza tastes good and it isn't very expensive.*

Students whose first language is not English can benefit from this social written language activity. The content of the text is not scripted, so students with limited language and written language skills can contribute to the activity and be part of the group.

| W6 | A Picture Is Worth a Thousand Words | Standards: 5, 7, 8, 12 |

Picture starters are a great way to help students increase their interest in a topic, as well as develop their descriptive vocabulary and content knowledge. Use pictures from magazines and newspapers of current events or social issues as topic starters. Students can also use a digital camera to take pictures of people and situations that interest them. Have the students print the pictures or post them on a personal or class web page. Productivity is increased when the author has an interest in the topic and when the author selects the topic on which he will write.

| W7 | Cut Up and Match Up | Standards: 1, 2, 3, 6, 11 |

Newspaper or magazine stories that contain lots of details can serve as good models for helping students learn how to organize information. Find a story in the newspaper or magazine that contains numerous details and that follows a chronological order. You might use an article in the local newspaper describing a recent school sporting event or an upcoming community event.

Cut the article into its parts, including the title, author's name and affiliation, paragraphs or sentences that relate the event, accompanying photographs, etc. Challenge individual students or groups of students to rearrange the article into its logical order. Have students read their articles aloud to verify the organization and logic. Discuss any variance in the sequence of the article's reordered events and lead students to understand why the details in the article need to be presented in a certain order.

| W8 | Post-Up Notes | Standards: 1, 2, 3, 6, 11 |

Collect some articles and photographs from the newspaper. Cut each photograph or story into two pieces, separating each story from its title and each picture from its caption. Put the body of each story and each photograph on a bulletin board and give students the titles and captions. Have the students read the information and match it with the appropriate article or photograph.

Story folders are a variation of this activity. Use double stick tape or Velcro® to attach the title of an article to the inside of a manila folder. Give students the parts of a newspaper story you have separated into its component parts (author, introductory paragraph, facts, summary paragraph). Have students use tape or Velcro® to attach the pieces of the story in order. Then have students read their completed story to the class. You can make the story folders available for students to read during free time, and students can also write alternative titles and introductory or summary paragraphs for their stories.

71

| W9 | You've Got Mail! | Standards: 1, 3, 4, 5, 6, 7, 8, 9, 10, 11, 12 |

E-mail can be a powerful tool to develop written language skills and to increase knowledge about people from different cultures. Begin by establishing individual or class e-mail accounts so students can regularly communicate with electronic pen pals (e-pals) all over the world. Below are some Internet sites that provide e-mail addresses for student pen pals. Adults should log on to each site, evaluate the site, and determine if its contents are appropriate. It is **imperative** that teachers and parents approve and monitor students' e-mail transmissions.

- Electronic Pen Pals
  http://www.surfnetkids.com/penpal.htm

- Pen Pal Box
  http://www.ks_connection.org/penpal/penpal.html

- EPALS Classroom Exchange
  http://www.epals.com

Have students research information about their e-pals' countries and cultures so it's easier to pose questions about those topics. Likewise, students will need to answer their e-pal's questions about themselves, including topics such as their favorite music or food and their hobbies and interests.

An e-mail letter is a form of personal communication, so don't worry about the structural form of the text. The capitalization, punctuation, and spelling don't have to be perfect. The goal of informal letter writing is to motivate students to write and to write frequently. The time required for structural alterations and the correction of spelling, grammar, and punctuation usually reduces the number of letter exchanges.

Structural Forms

Some educators spend too much instructional time trying to perfect students' handwriting. Students practice and practice the slant of a letter's line, the size of the loop at the top of a letter, and the length of the letter's "tail." Students need to know how to consistently write manuscript or cursive letters so that others can read them, and they need to write letters fluently. Excessive time spent on perfecting loops and curves, however, is time that should be spent on generating ideas, organizing thoughts, and transferring them into text.

While some students may be spending too much time perfecting their handwriting, there are others who do not consistently write letters that can be read or discerned one from another. Some students erase and erase their attempts at forming letters until there is a hole in the paper. For these students, multisensory handwriting activities are appropriate. Some students who have significant difficulty with fine motor control may benefit from working with an occupational therapist.

Teachers may need to consider using technology to accommodate students who have significant fine-motor weaknesses. Have students routinely use computers in the classroom and at home to acquire information and to complete assignments. All students need to acquire basic computing skills and to have regular opportunities to use them, and this is particularly true for students who have problems with written language.

| W10 | Don't Worry About the Lines | Standard: 4 |

The purpose of this activity is to teach correct letter formations and to have students freely write letters. Letter formation and writing fluency are often promoted by providing students with media other than traditional lined paper. You might have students begin to form letters by walking over 6-foot letter formations taped out on the floor. Then they can progress to finger tracing 24-inch raised letters made on poster board (with puff paint or glue). Next have them trace 6-8 inch letters on unlined notebook paper. Finally, have them write on ruled notebook paper. Anxiety about handwriting can be reduced when students write letters without the constraint of "staying between the lines."

| W11 | Number Rhymes | Standard: 4 |

Teach students to rhyme as they write numbers. The combination of verbal rhyme and motor movement helps students with learning problems remember the sequential multi-step movements necessary to form each number. Some number rhymes are listed on the next page.

- **0** Around we go, that's the way to make zero.
- **1** One is fun, top to bottom is the way to make a one.
- **2** Around and back one-two, that's the way to make a two.
- **3** Around and around a tree, that's the way to make a three.
- **4** Down and over and down some more, top to bottom, that's the way to make a four.
- **5** Across, down and around you dive, that's the way to make a five.
- **6** Down and roll the mix, that's the way to make a six.
- **7** Across the sky and down from heaven, that's the way to make a seven.
- **8** Make an S but don't wait, that's the way to make an eight.
- **9** A hoop and a line, that's the way to make a nine.

W12	Dot-to-Dot	Standard: 4

Uppercase and lowercase letters are written by beginning the stroke in different places on the paper. Some letters have "tails" and go below the line while others reach up and touch the top line. Use verbal prompts and visual cues to help students begin and end letters in the correct location on their papers. Colors are a great visual cue because colors can convey meaning. For example, you might use a stoplight as a visual cue. The green light or green color means "go" or "start," yellow means "slow down and look where you are going," and red means "stop" or "finished." Cue a student with those "stoplight words" to provide feedback and coach him as he forms letters.

You might have students follow a sequence of dotted lines, that when connected, form a letter. Mark the beginning and ending location of the letter's dotted lines with the appropriate color (green for the beginning, red for the ending), and add direction lines if necessary. You can also present numbered sequences of dots for students to follow. Here are a couple of examples of dot-to-dot letters.

W13	**VAKT Clues**	Standard: 4

Visual, auditory, kinesthetic, and tactile (VAKT) cues for handwriting can be used to help students learn basic letter formation. Here are some steps for applying VAKT to handwriting instruction:

1. Write the letter with a marker or crayon while the student observes.
2. Say the name of the letter together with the student.
3. The student traces the letter with a finger while simultaneously saying the name of the letter. Have the student do this correctly at least three times.
4. The student copies and names the letter correctly at least three times.
5. The student writes and names the letter correctly without looking at the model.

You can form the letter in materials that have an exaggerated texture to heighten the kinesthetic and tactile experience for the student. For example, you can trace a letter with glue and cover it with rice, grits, or sand. Once dried, have a student trace the texture-enhanced letter with his finger. As the student traces the textured letter, he describes the motion. Your student might say, "Start at the bottom line and slant to the right until I touch the top line. Curve to the left forming a small loop. Curve back to the right and cross the first slanted line. Keep curving the line until I touch the bottom line. I wrote a cursive **S**."

W14	**What's In a Name?**	Standards: 3, 4, 5, 6, 9, 10, 12

This activity helps students understand the importance of vocabulary and grammatical sentence structure. Begin by cutting out interesting pictures from magazines or newspapers or have students take pictures of scenes at home and school with a digital camera. Display the pictures in the classroom. Have each student write a title for each picture. As a class, discuss the titles and their relation to the meanings of the pictures.

Here are some variations of this basic activity:
- Have students write titles that are informative, argumentative, persuasive, or descriptive.
- Provide titles and have students match them to their corresponding pictures. Ambiguous titles will provide a variety of matches and points for discussion.
- Have students fill in the blank of a caption with a missing word or phrase.

For students who speak English as a second language or who have limited English proficiency, you might make the following alterations to the activity:
- Translate a title that is written in their native language into English. Discuss the grammatical differences between the titles.
- Have them write synonyms for words found in the title.
- Have them correctly fill in the blank with an English word that completes a title.

| W15 | **Speech-to-Text** | Standard: 8 |

Computer hardware and software are evolving every day. Speech-to-text features are becoming more commonplace, and this feature is particularly interesting for those individuals who have written language difficulties. Instead of using the computer's keyboard to type individual letters and words, an individual speaks into a microphone, and the computer types what that individual says — speech-to-text. This technology supports students as they learn correct spelling and grammatical structures. It also eliminates laborious handwriting and takes advantage of the student's oral language skills. Some helpful websites for information about speech recognition include the following:

- *Apple Speech Technologies:* http://www.apple.com/macos/speech
- *Dragon Systems:* http://www.dragonsys.com
- *Nuance:* http://www.nuance.com

| W16 | **How Did the Expert Do It?** | Standards: 1, 2, 3, 4, 5, 6, 9 |

A model is an ideal pattern to follow. People use models to learn or to improve upon something they produce. You can use models from various expert writers to help students learn about mood, distinguish between fact and fiction, appreciate imagery, etc.

Select a wide variety of literature and have your students read passages from different authors that fit the goals of your current instruction. Have students circle words or phrases that are examples of the lesson's objective, such as figurative language, symbolism, or dialog. Have students read the circled words to the class and discuss how the examples meet the objective.

Encourage individual students or groups of students to provide alternative word choices or phrases to the circled words. Then have them rewrite the expert's passage using their own examples. Finally, have students compare their passages with the expert's original passage and discuss similarities and differences in style.

| W17 | **Graphic Organizers** | Standards: 4, 5, 7, 8, 12 |

E.M. Forster, a British author, is quoted as saying, "How can I know what I think until I see what I say?" Visual organizers help writers organize information. Organizers come in as many varieties and forms as do writers. The type of writing can determine the choice of form for the organizer. A timeline or linear organizer is a useful format for topics that are highly sequential. A web or a topic organizer can be used when there are several related categories for one topic, or when specific information about a topic needs to be discussed. There are many software programs available to help students create graphic organizers.

Some examples of graphic organizers are shown on the next page. See activity **C11** (page 93) for other ideas for using graphic organizers.

76

Sequential Organizer

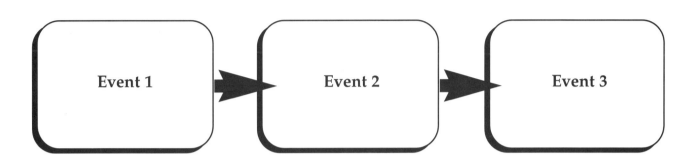

Topic Organizer

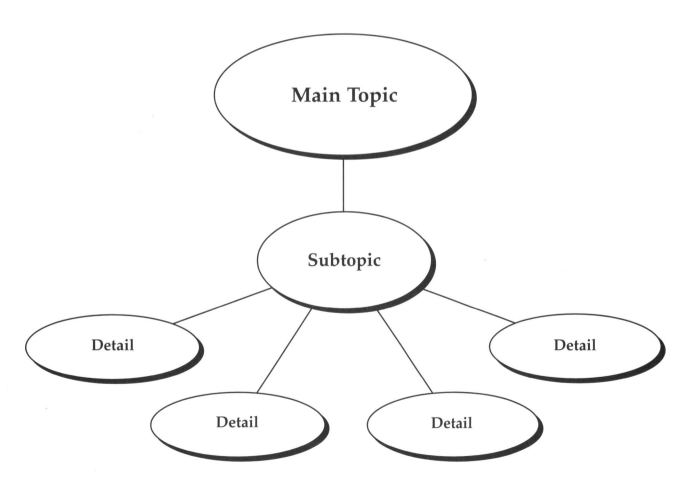

| W18 | I Need to See It — Let Me Write It | Standards: 5, 6 |

Have you ever had someone ask you a question like, "How do you spell *thesaurus*?" You think a minute and then begin spelling, "thes . . . thesarsus . . . Wait a minute. Let me write it. I'll know if it's spelled correctly if I see it." You write the word *thesarus* and you realize it is misspelled. You know it's misspelled because the word *doesn't look right*. Students can learn to correctly spell words by writing them in a variety of ways. Here are some strategies you can help them use:

- Complete the word when a random letter is omitted.

  ✔ d i n __ s a u r

  ✔ d i n o s a __ r

- Scramble the letters in the word and have the student correctly write the word.

  ✔ s r a u d n i o

- Complete a sentence by filling in the blank with a word from a word list.

  ✔ T-Rex is the fiercest _____ of the meat-eating group.

Caution: Observe students as they complete an assignment that requires them to *write each word five times*. Many students mindlessly go through the motion of copying words. Do not use just one type of writing activity as a way to help students learn how to spell words. A variety of activities will maintain their motivation and promote generalization.

78

Revising, Editing, and Publishing

This category of the writing process is probably the only one readers ever see. Writers revise as they write. They change a word in a sentence to improve clarity; they add words to better describe. The purpose of revision is to change — not correct. The purpose of editing is to correct. Writers edit or proof their work to find and correct errors. Students with learning problems are not good editors because they lack the skills or the risk-taking behaviors required for editing. Publishing is when the written text is made available for viewing. The teacher may only view the text, or it may be available for thousands of people to read, depending on the method of publication.

W19	**What Did I Say?**	Standards: 4, 5, 8, 10

Talking word processors and word prediction programs provide auditory feedback to the writer because the student hears what he has written. Students who speak English as a second language or who have limited English proficiency might greatly benefit from talking word processors. Text-to-speech programs provide many benefits beyond auditory feedback, including identification of spelling and grammatical errors. You can also have students use specific vocabulary to generate simple or complex sentences. A search of the Internet will provide you with the names of several text-to-speech software packages, including *Write:OutLoud* and *Co:Writer 4000*.

W20	**E-help**	Standards: 4, 5, 8, 10

There are many electronic programs and devices that help writers revise and edit their written text. Most of these programs use color codes to highlight misspellings, agrammatical sentence structures, and words that might be used incorrectly. Some programs underline misspelled words with a red wavy line and underline agrammatical sentence structures and punctuation errors with a green wavy line. Some editing programs beep immediately after the writer incorrectly types a word.

Students who are bilingual or who have limited English proficiency might benefit from revision programs and activities. Revision activities that target vocabulary development and grammatical structures can be individualized to meet the student's specific needs. Teachers and writers can adopt color codes to identify words and sentence structures that can be revised or that require editing.

Students can also benefit from small, portable electronic devices that specialize in revision and editing functions. Electronic spell checkers, thesauruses, dictionaries, and grammar checkers are practical tools for all students, especially for students who have problems with written language. These devices are especially useful for students who are bilingual or who have limited English proficiency.

The **Revising** exercises on page 84 will help writers and editors learn visual revision codes. Discuss the students' revisions and the effect the changes have on the meaning of the sentence.

| W21 | **Backward Editing** | Standards: 4, 5, 6 |

Writers have difficulty recognizing and correcting their own text because of *executive knowledge* — knowledge of the text that only the writer possesses. Executive knowledge interferes with editing because writers "know what they meant to say" and don't recognize many of their own errors. For this reason, expert writers ask others to proofread their writing. Other people usually identify mistakes the author often overlooks.

Backward editing interferes with executive knowledge because the meaning of the text is interrupted. Sentences don't exist because sentence structure is eliminated, and the meaning of the text is disrupted. The student is forced to proofread individual words.

Ask students to begin editing their text at the end of the piece rather than at the beginning. Another backward strategy requires students to edit their text moving from the right margin to the left rather than from left to right.

| W22 | **Editors as Risk Takers** | Standards: 4, 5, 6 |

Many students with learning disabilities lack the knowledge and skills to edit their own written texts. They rely on their teachers to identify and correct their errors. Students' dependence on others to edit their work contributes to learned helplessness and poor risk-taking behaviors. Initially, teachers should give students encouragement and positive reinforcement for attempting to edit, regardless of the success of their attempts.

Ask students to circle words, punctuation marks, or sentences they think might contain errors. Different-colored ink can be used to denote each type of error. For example, red circled words indicate ones students think are misspelled, green circled punctuation marks are ones students think may be incorrect, and blue circles placed around entire sentences indicate that the student thinks it might contain a grammar error.

As a variation, have student editors write the number of errors they think they might find on that line in the margin. The editor could also indicate the type of error(s) by using letter codes to represent the error. Here's an example:

2   I saw five float in the parad today.

         (2 unspecified errors could be found in the sentence.)

Or

1-G and 1-S   I saw five float in the parad today.

         (1-G indicates 1 Grammar error — five float (omitted **s** plural)
         (1-S indicates 1 spelling error — parad/parade)

You can expand this activity by having the student editors correct the errors. Initially, you can reinforce the student's *attempt* to correct rather than the *accuracy* of the correction. Concentrate on editing of specific errors, or reinforce a broader application of skills to include all types of written errors.

| W23 | **Four Eyes and Ears** | Standards: 3, 4, 5, 6 |

Authors can have difficulty evaluating the clarity of meaning in their own writing. A pair of unfamiliar eyes and ears can often identify confusing or unclear meaning in another's writing. Have young authors ask a peer, or someone unfamiliar with the writing assignment or text, to silently or orally read their written text. The reader should stop whenever he is confused about the meaning of a passage, or whenever he has a revision or editing suggestion. The writer should also stop the reader whenever he hears something that does not fit with the intended meaning. Have the writer immediately revise or edit the passage.

| W24 | **Hot Off the Press** | Standards: 4, 5, 6, 8, 9, 11, 12 |

The publication of written text is the culmination of the writing process. There are a variety of publication formats writers and readers can explore, including books, newspapers, and newsletters. The style and format of the text may be dictated by the publication's format. For example, newspapers are typically published in columns, whereas newsletters may or may not be published in columns. Work that appears in a publication, or even the format of a publication, emphasizes the importance of writing. Readers' responses to publications generally motivate writers to continue writing, which is the ultimate goal for teachers who work with students who have problems with written language.

You can publish students' works in a collection of formats using a variety of publishing tools. Examples of print or electronic publications include the following:

- Monthly classroom newsletters for distribution to parents, which can include articles about different cultures and geographical regions, and interviews with students from different cultural and linguistic backgrounds
- Weekly school newsletters for distribution to the school's students, faculty, and parents, or via a classroom website
- Book reports for display in the classroom or school library
- Research reports for class discussion or debate club topics
- Entries in literary fairs

81

Reference

Louisiana State Department of Education (1998). Teaching strategies and student accommodations. *General education access guide.*

Resource

May, C. H. (1997). *Tales have been told: activities for higher level syntax.* Eau Claire, WI: Thinking Publications.

The book contains nine lessons that utilize folk tales from various countries and cultures to teach map skills, vocabulary, story grammar and story mapping, passive voice and adjective clauses.

The LD Teacher's Language Arts Companion:
A Multisensory Approach   82

The 5 Ws

Answer each question. Be sure to ask your teacher for any information you need to complete the chart.

Name:		Date:
Who	Who am I writing for?	
	Who can I work with?	
	Who will read my final product?	
What	What is the topic?	
	What does the audience know about the topic?	
	What's the purpose of the writing?	
	What resources can be used?	
	What reference style is required?	
When	When is the first draft due?	
	When is the final copy due?	
Where	Where will the final product be seen?	
	Where can I find references?	
How	How does it have to look?	
	How many paragraphs does it have to have?	
	How many pages does it have to be?	
	How will it be graded?	

83

Revising

Name _____

Read each item. Rewrite each sentence, replacing each underlined word or phrase with something of your own. Did the meaning change or stay the same? The first one is done for you.

1. He was <u>going for the home run ball</u>!

   He was trying to hit a home run.
   _____

2. The <u>young boy</u> helplessly looked over the battlefield.

   _____

3. Many of the soldiers <u>jumped</u> from the plane.

   _____

4. Ballerinas <u>spun</u> on toe shoes.

   _____

5. How much <u>should I put in</u>?

   _____

6. He used his <u>head</u> to solve that problem.

   _____

7. We were <u>totally mystified</u> by what happened.

   _____

8. My friends were <u>very thankful</u> that they got a ride home.

   _____

9. The chili tasted <u>regular</u>.

   _____

10. We <u>enjoyed</u> the park. It was a <u>lot of fun</u>!

    _____

6 Content Area Skills

Succeeding in content area subjects such as social studies, math, science, and literature requires that students develop many skills, including these:

- decoding and understanding new vocabulary words (that often represent major concepts)
- comprehending expository text
- conducting research on diverse topics, with and without the aid of technology
- using study skills to learn, remember, and use new information

To perform these tasks, students must be able to read, write, spell, speak, and listen effectively. They also need to be able to visually represent concepts through avenues such as drama; sketching; painting; graphs and charts; and technology presentations. In addition, each content area has vocabulary specific to it. For example, *denominator*, *fraction*, and *equation* have very specific meanings in mathematics; *element*, *photosynthesis*, and *combustion* are specific to science; and *genre*, *style*, and *mood* are important in literature.

Students with learning disabilities need multisensory activities to master content area skills and concepts, as well as research and study skills. If content area teachers want students to be successful, they must teach students language arts, research, and study skills simultaneously with content. The activities in this chapter are designed with that purpose in mind. Many of the activities in other chapters of this book can be applied to content area subjects as well.

Goals

- To organize for effective studying
- To locate a variety of resources to meet specific needs
- To use print and nonprint resources effectively
- To use appropriate research and study strategies
- To communicate about content area learning in different ways
- To collaborate with others to do research and learn
- To master content area skills and concepts

| C1 | **Getting Organized** | Standards: 4, 8, 12 |

Students with learning disabilities usually need help with external organization before they can even begin to learn. Following are some examples of things you can guide your students to do to organize themselves in a multisensory manner:

- Use colored book covers, folders, tabs, and dots to color code textbooks, notebooks, and other supplies according to subject area.
- Prepare a morning book bag and an afternoon book bag.
- Keep a detailed calendar with important events and project due dates. Look at the calendar, touch important dates, and go over them aloud once a day or more.
- Keep visual checklists for classwork and homework. Go over these aloud daily. Check off accomplished tasks.
- Make timelines or flowcharts of steps for getting special projects done.
- Tape record directions for procedures and projects. Refer to the tape as needed.
- Highlight and put a box around key words and directions in handouts. Read highlights aloud. Practice directions under teacher supervision.
- Set aside time each evening to organize for the next school day.
- Schedule time for rest and extracurricular activities, as well as studying.

Some students are motivated by using an electronic organizer to keep up-to-date calendars and lists. However, make sure that they remember to refer to their organizers at preset times.

Because organization can be so overwhelming, students can set one main goal (keep my desk neat, get the right books to each class, remember all of my homework) for each grading period. Use the **Getting Organized** sheet on page 106 to make goal-setting more concrete for students.

| C2 | **Instructing Students** | Standards: 3, 4, 9, 10, 11 |

It's important to be aware of the needs of students with learning disabilities as you provide instruction. Make instruction as multisensory as possible, and teach them in the ways they learn best. Here are some guidelines:

- Sit students near the focal point of instruction.
- Write your objectives on the board. Go over them orally before the lesson to set purposes for learning and after the lesson for closure.
- Organize your instruction. Before beginning, use a visual outline as you explain how the lesson is organized. Use colored chalk, transparency pens, or ink to help students see the organization.
- Break instruction down into smaller sections, and teach one section at a time.
- Use visual aides such as charts, pictures, and maps.

- Use concrete objects and hands-on experiences to teach concepts.
- Eliminate unnecessary information or talk.
- Have students restate often what they are learning in their own words.
- Use a variety of teaching methods that fit all learning modalities.
- Provide a photocopy of overhead transparencies if copying is a problem.
- If note-taking is a problem, allow students to duplicate your notes, or ask a peer to take notes on carbonless duplicating paper so that notes can be shared. This allows students with note-taking problems to concentrate on listening and learning rather than taking notes. Another option is to let students do modified note-taking. Give them an outline of your lesson plan and let them fill in details during the lesson. Call their attention to details as you come to them.
- When you ask questions, allow increased response time, or inform students of questions you will ask them ahead of time so that they may develop and practice their answers.
- Provide assignments in advance so students can spend extra time on them.
- Shorten required reading and/or writing tasks if these are areas of weakness. If the learning problem is in mathematics, remember it is better for students to do a few problems right than a lot of problems wrong.
- If oral reading is a problem, give students prior notice of passages you will ask them to read so they can practice them.
- Provide review sheets. Use color-coded paper to organize the sheets according to subjects or topics.
- Assign students to study groups to review material.
- Coping with learning disabilities can be very exhausting, so allow frequent rest breaks.
- If you have bilingual students, use vocabulary words from their native language when giving directions or introducing topics, or let these students teach you and the rest of the class relevant terms using their first language. That way, everyone benefits and enjoys learning more!

C3	Projects	Standards: 3, 4, 9

Sometimes students with learning disabilities surprise their teachers. Often they appear to be on the right track with a project but hand in something that is unacceptable when the project is due. Many times this is because they understood the directions differently from the way you intended. Other times it is because they do not express themselves well in writing (if the project is a written report), or they do not express themselves well orally (if the project is a speech).

Follow guidelines such as these to help your students complete projects of which they can be proud:

- List written directions for projects in numerical order rather than in paragraphs.
- Provide visual cues for written directions through photos or illustrations.
- Go over directions for projects as students read the directions. Paraphrase the written directions. Then have students explain the directions to you.
- Show concrete examples to illustrate what you want students to do.
- Post directions for projects where students can refer to them again and again. Individual project sheets are a good idea.
- Allow another student to rephrase or reteach directions to those who have difficulty understanding.
- Break projects down into smaller parts, and confer with students as they finish each part. Have students use a checklist to mark off each part as they finish.
- Provide time for students to discuss their projects with each other. It helps students to hear what classmates are doing.
- Rather than documenting projects only through written reports or speeches, allow students to demonstrate what they have learned through creative means, such as puppet shows, skits, timelines, models, dioramas, and videos. Help students respect and value diverse ways of communicating knowledge.

| C4 | **Team Work** | Standards: 4, 9, 10, 11, 12 |

Students benefit when they do research and study content together in cooperative groups. Not only does working with each other motivate students, but it also requires them to do the following:

- communicate clearly
- accept and appreciate diversity (points of view, language, culture)
- think critically and creatively
- cooperate with others to meet goals
- expand social roles

Working with each other is naturally multisensory because students must use verbal and nonverbal means to communicate. You can facilitate additional use of the senses and movement by using multisensory instructional techniques, teaching multisensory study skills, and requiring multi-modal presentations of learning. Many of the activities in this chapter lend themselves to teamwork. Doing these activities in groups is especially good for bilingual students because it allows them to learn to use English in casual settings.

C5 | Readability of Texts | Standards: 1, 3, 6, 8, 10

It is important to adopt textbooks with bold headings, numerous visual aides to illustrate ideas, and clear organization. You should also pay attention to the difficulty of the vocabulary words and sentence structures. You may, however, find that textbooks that are on the appropriate readability level for most of the class can still be on a reading level that is too difficult for students with language disabilities. You may also find that students for whom English is a second language have problems reading their textbooks because of a language barrier. Here are some ideas for providing information in other ways:

- Duplicate information about the topic from a book with a lower reading level. If the information came from a textbook on a lower grade level, be sure to remove all evidence of the grade level.
- Write a summary of the text in easier words for the students to study.
- Audiotape your summary so students can listen to it again and again.
- Show a videotape that teaches the concepts. Let students watch it over and over.
- Investigate computer software or Internet sites that teach the text material.
- Allow students to read with a classmate so that stronger readers can help weaker ones.
- Let students follow along as you or a volunteer reads the text to them. (You can tape record this reading so students can listen more than once.)

C6 | Chunking of Reading Assignments | Standard: 3

Students often become frustrated or panicky when they are faced with long content area reading assignments. You can guide these students to break the assignments into manageable chunks (several pages with a definite beginning and ending). Have them cut colorful sticky notes into strips and place a strip between each chunk. They might chunk the information by a set number of pages or use headings within chapters as guides. Whenever students come to a strip of paper, have them stop reading and summarize what they have learned so far. Then they should get up and take a short break or give themselves a small reward.

Provide each student with a copy of the **Reading Assignments** chart on page 107 to keep track of reading progress.

| C7 | **Book Parts** | Standards: 1, 3 |

Understanding the parts of a content area textbook will help students know how to use it effectively. Rather than just having your students turn to the title page, the table of contents, index, glossary, and so forth, have them mark book parts with colorful sticky notes with a different color representing each part. Also, have them write the purpose(s) of each book part on each sticky note. For example, on the glossary note, students can write "to find definitions" and "to look up exact spellings." Some students might find it helpful to write purposes in question form for each book part. For example, they might write, "What topics are covered in this book?" and "What page numbers are topics found on?" for the table of contents. Using the same color key and note format for every textbook will help students find book parts quickly and use them more efficiently.

| C8 | **Text Features** | Standards: 1, 3 |

Students need to look within a text to note how it is organized. They might ask themselves the following questions as they look over the text:
- Are headings and subheadings used?
- Are vocabulary words in boldface?
- Are new words defined in the margins?
- Are there study questions at the end of each section of text or only at the end of each chapter?
- Is there a graphic organizer provided at the beginning of the text?
- Are there other graphics such as maps or charts?

In order to make the above considerations more multisensory for students, have them color-code text features using colored stick-on dots in each chapter before reading. They can place different-colored dots for such features as headings, subheadings, graphics, vocabulary words, etc. Post the key for the colored dots in a prominent place and refer to them often to remind students how to use text features to learn.

| C9 | **Text Structures** | Standards: 1, 3 |

If students can identify types of text structures, they know what to expect, can predict the text, and apply appropriate comprehension strategies. When teaching types of text structures (cause/effect, compare/contrast, time, descriptive), teach signal words (*because, as a result, before, after, like*) to give students clues as to the text structure.

Post these signal words under the corresponding text structure title on a bulletin board. Put words for different structures in different colors. When students come to the signal words in text, have them underline those words with the indicated color. After the first reading, have students reread the sentences with the signal words aloud and use the color-code as a clue to identify the text structure. Be sure to emphasize that signal words are only clues, and some signal words can indicate more than one type of text. Students must read the text critically to correctly identify the structure for certain. Use a **Text Structure** chart like the one on the following page to introduce signal words to your students.

Text Structure

Cause-Effect
(relates cause to outcomes)

because

as a result

since

consequently

therefore

so that

Time
(tells time-order)

on

before

after

when

then

next

Comparison-Contrast
(tells how things are alike and different)

like

while

on the other hand

similarly

however

yet

Descriptive
(describes)

for example

most important

for instance

in fact

also

furthermore

C10	Adapting Reading Rates	Standards: 1, 3

All good readers adapt their reading rates according to their purposes and the difficulty of the material. Many students with learning disabilities, however, tend to read everything word by word at the same rate. To help students practice adapting reading rates, try the following strategies.

- Select interesting materials for students to read for different purposes. Here are some examples of reading materials you might provide for your students:
  - ✔ *Movie listings from the local paper* — Have students locate the time/location of a movie they want to see.
  - ✔ *Menus from popular restaurants* — Have students locate foods they like, foods that are prepared a certain way, and prices they can afford.
  - ✔ *Brochures for vacations, vehicles, summer camps, or sports equipment* — Have students decide how to spend an imagined jackpot of money.
  - ✔ *Assembly instructions for furniture, bicycle, etc. or software installation instructions* — Have students practice reading carefully to follow directions. (Have them act out assembling or installing.)
  - ✔ *Sunday comics* — Have students read for entertainment.
  - ✔ *Short section of a content area textbook* — Have students read to prepare for a quiz.

- Model with exaggerated eye and body movements how to read each selection. Share your thought processes aloud as you do so. Here are some examples of reading strategies and ways to present them:
  - *Scanning* — Draw your finger and eyes quickly down a column as you seek a piece of information; then read more slowly after you find the information.
  - *Skimming* — Move your finger and your eyes back and forth quickly; notice chapter titles, headings, graphics, introductions, and conclusions.
  - *Reading carefully* — Point to and look at every phrase or word, reread when necessary, stop to look at charts or graphs, and ask yourself questions to check comprehension.

- Have students practice reading the selections you provide using the exaggerated movements themselves. Lead them to adjust their reading rates for different purposes. For example, instruct them to read more slowly and carefully when they are reading instructions, encourage them to skim when they are reading a menu, and have them select their own rate when they read for enjoyment. Later have them practice the exaggerated movements as they begin reading new materials for different purposes. Most students will gradually stop doing the exaggerated movements on their own as they gain comfort with adapting reading rates. Others may need the exaggerated movements for quite some time to adapt rate in a multisensory manner.

92

C11 | Graphic Organizers   Standards: 1, 3

Students can use graphic organizers (visual representations of text) to organize ideas before, during, and after reading. Graphic organizers can take many forms. They can be simple outlines with headings (main ideas) and subheadings (supporting details) or Venn diagrams that show how concepts are alike and different. Flow charts, concept trees, timelines, or any other visual representation that makes sense to students make excellent graphic organizers. Here is an example of a cause and effect concept tree:

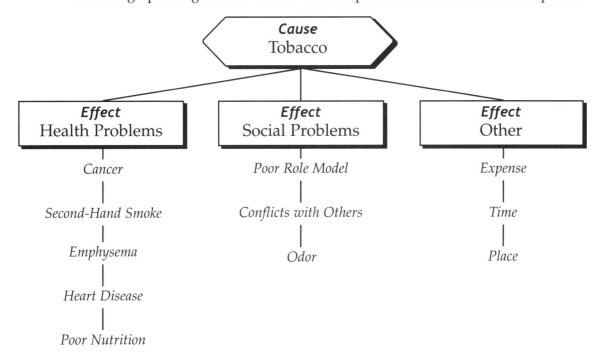

With a little imagination, any graphic organizer can be made multisensory. In the above example, you could prepare the graphic organizer ahead of time with these modifications:

- Write the cause (Tobacco) on a red note card.
- Write the broad effects (Health Problems, Social Problems, Other) on blue note cards.
- Write the specific effects on yellow note cards.

Have the students use the note cards to assemble the graphic organizer before reading to predict what they will be learning. After reading, have students move the cards as necessary to make corrections. Later, mix up the cards so that students can put the organizer back together for review.

After experiencing your graphic organizers, have students construct their own for new text using note cards, sentence strips, or construction paper. They can exchange organizers with each other to check understanding and study for tests. As always, make sure that their graphic organizers are correct before letting them study.

See activity **W17** on page 76 for other information on the use of graphic organizers.

C12	**Mapping the Library**	Standards: 4, 7, 8, 11

Students with learning disabilities often have a hard time finding their way around new places. Many times, they also have problems remembering simple directions for performing tasks. Those factors can make using the library a difficult chore. Take your students to the library for a brief, initial visit to get a general feel for the place. Next, take some simple steps to make library use easier in the future:

- Help students draw a map of the school library.
- Help them label the map with map flags and color it with different colors representing different areas. Highlight the most commonly used areas.
- Using the map, let students talk about and model where to go in the library for different purposes. (Don't forget to include the Help Desk in your discussion.)
- Discuss and model how to check out books, use card catalogs (electronic or non-electronic), work duplicating machines and other equipment, and so forth. Have students practice the procedures using simple props, such as student-made library cards, map of library sketched on the floor with masking tape, cardboard boxes with buttons/levers drawn on them, etc.

When students visit the library again, encourage them to visualize their map and simulated procedures. After the visit, discuss and model any modifications they want to make to the map or ways they think that procedures can be improved.

C13	**Response Cards**	Standards: 2, 3, 4, 7, 10

Having students use response cards to answer questions in class instead of answering individually allows all students to participate and lets you monitor understanding of the entire class at once. Provide students with large note cards and markers and let them make their own response cards. As you ask questions or call out terms, students hold up the appropriate card. Use the cards in multiple ways, such as these:

- Students can hold up cards with <, >, or = to answer questions about number relationships.
- Students can hold up cards with *before* or *after* to indicate the sequence of events you list.
- Students can hold up cards with *solid*, *liquid*, or *gas* to classify types of matter.
- Students can hold up cards with *fable*, *folk tale*, *poetry*, and *science fiction* to classify genres of literature.
- Students can hold up cards with *yes* or *no* to indicate answers to any dichotomous question such as, "Is this animal (*bear, trout, firefly*) a mammal?" or "Is this heavenly body (*Jupiter, sun, moon*) a planet?"
- Students can hold up cards with *atlas*, *encyclopedia*, or *almanac* to indicate where to go to research specific questions.
- Have bilingual students use their native language on one side of their response cards and English on the other.

You can make this activity even more multisensory by writing the item(s) students are responding to (*bear, trout, firefly*) on the board or a card so students can see it as you say it.

C14	Multisensory Study	Standards: 1, 3

Multisensory strategies will help students master math, science, social studies, language arts, or other content. Have your students follow the easy steps below as they study:

1. With your help, the student goes through the text and highlights the most important parts. If students are not allowed to write in books, have them use sticky notes with arrows drawn on.

2. The student discusses the important parts of the text with a teacher or a peer to ensure basic understanding.

3. The student or someone else reads the most important parts of the text into a tape recorder.

4. While listening to the tape (several times if necessary), the student reads the highlighted parts of the text.

5. The student puts the title of key terms and principles on the front of a note card. (Glue may be used to raise the letters.) The definitions or explanations are written on the back in the student's own words. The student reads each term or principle into the tape recorder while tracing or skywriting. Next, the student reads the corresponding definition or explanation.

6. The student uses the tape recording and cards to see, say, hear, and touch while studying.

7. To check understanding, the student can turn off the tape to explain the terms and principles.

C15	Content Area Games	Standards: 1, 3, 7, 9, 10, 11

Games are a natural way to use multiple senses and movement in order to learn. Most popular games can be adapted to fit content areas. Follow these steps to create your own "Social Studies Jeopardy":

1. Prepare an overhead transparency or game board with categories (history, climate, geography, literature, fine arts, culture, miscellaneous) written across the top and 100, 200, 300, 400, and 500 written in the columns under each category.

2. Write five questions for each category, ranging from easiest to most difficult.

3. Have students or teams take turns choosing a category and level of question. The 100-point questions in a category are the easiest, moving up in difficulty to the 500-point questions, which are hardest.

4. Read the question. If the students answer correctly, give them a chip or play money that represents the number of points received. If an incorrect answer is given, it is someone else's turn to choose a category and question level.

5. The person or team with the most points at the end of the game wins.

95

A variation of this game is to leave the category titles blank. As students answer questions at various levels of difficulty, they also try to guess the category title for additional points.

Another variation is to have groups of students collaborate to research a geographic region assigned to them. They can then develop categories, questions, and answers for their geographic regions. Have groups take turns playing each other's games.

Students who were born in other regions or have relatives living in other countries enjoy making games about their homelands. Bilingual students can make language one of the categories to teach the class simple terms in a foreign language. For more game ideas that can be adapted to content areas, see activity **R30** on page 52.

C16 | Songs, Rhymes, and Mnemonics — Standard: 3

Many students learn better if the information they need to learn is put into a song or rhyme. The music and rhythm helps them commit new learning to long-term memory. Often songs and rhymes make use of mnemonics or memory tricks. Examples include *Roy G Biv* to remember the colors of the rainbow (red, orange, yellow, green, blue, indigo, violet) and *Every Good Boy Does Fine* (E-G-B-D-F) to remember the lines on the treble clef.

There are commercial products available that teach months of the year, colors, and math facts using mnemonics, songs, and rhymes. You can make up your own songs, rhymes, and mnemonics that are specific to your learning situation (important dates or people, food pyramid, parts of the body). Increase the relevance of the activity by having students work cooperatively to create their own songs and rhymes. Notice that many adults still use songs, rhymes, and mnemonics they learned as children (*Thirty days hath September . . .*) for rote memory tasks.

C17 | Reciprocal Teaching — Standards: 3, 4, 7, 11, 12

Many people learn a concept or skill best by teaching it to someone else. Follow these steps to give your students opportunities to engage in reciprocal teaching:
1. Two students research different questions about the same topic.
2. Each student plans a way to teach the other person what he or she has learned. (Emphasize that the teaching technique should be more than just "telling." It can include photos, diagrams, simple models, mnemonics, doing an experiment, and other multisensory methods.)
3. The students take turns teaching each other. They continue until they are sure each one understands the other's material.
4. Pair the first partnership of students with another partnership (who researched a different question) so the two partnerships can teach each other.
5. Have the foursome prepare a short demonstration of the main points they learned. Demonstrations can include making a poster, doing a skit, creating a song, or any other creative mode of presentation.

| C18 | **Learning Line** | **Standards: 2, 3, 4** |

A learning line is a visual representation that communicates content area concepts. You can make a learning line by stretching a nylon rope across the front of the room and placing colorful clothespins on it. You can then clip related curriculum-relevant material to the clothespins. Here are some ideas for using a learning line to express mathematical concepts:

- Prepare cards with numerals for younger students to pin to the learning line in sequential order.
- Make cards with decimals or fractions (.1, 1/10, 4/5) to be sequenced for older students.
- Provide cards with >, <, =, and other mathematical signs for students to express mathematical relationships.
- Cut circles into fractional parts for comparisons.

You can also run your learning line vertically, from the floor to the ceiling, which allows the class to use the line in many other ways. You might also use a combination of a horizontal learning line with vertical lines extending below. Here are some examples of content you can place on learning lines:

- In history class, place events in chronological order.
- In computer class, sequence directions for using search engines.
- In science, show classifications of animals. (See the example below.)
- In health, categorize foods according to the food pyramid.
- In English, list characteristics of genres of literature or classify pieces of literature according to their genres.

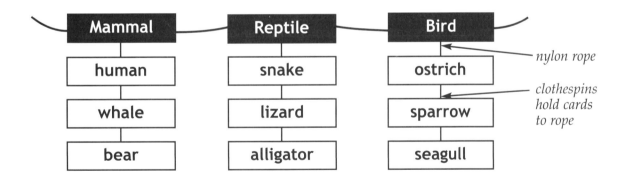

| C19 | **Communicating Mathematics** | Standards: 1, 4, 7, 8 |

All too often, students do their math work in silence and isolation. This is a mistake because communicating mathematical ideas makes math multisensory and makes learning easier. Try the following suggestions to make math a multisensory experience for your students:

- Put students in groups to solve mathematical tasks. Have them explain the task and the solution orally to each other and the class. Encourage them to visually represent the task and solution.

- Have students read math word problems aloud to each other. Then encourage students to diagram the word problems or find ways to act them out.

- Have students keep math journals in which they use words, numerals, and drawings to do the following:
  ✔ Explain how they worked a math exercise.
  ✔ Describe a difficulty they are having with a math procedure.
  ✔ Write about how they will use math skills and concepts in daily life.
  ✔ Develop a math word problem (with solution) for classmates to work.

- Have students share their journals with each other. At different points in the semester, ask them to look back over their journals to discuss their progress.

- Have students research famous mathematicians and mathematical theories using the library and the Internet. Let them make posters that summarize their findings.

| C20 | **Specialized Language** | Standard: 3 |

Understanding content area books and exercises can be especially problematic for students with learning disabilities because of the special language involved. It is a good idea to call attention to signs, symbols, and other types of special language in multisensory ways. Here are some examples:

- When working addition, subtraction, multiplication, and division problems, have students say and trace the +, – , x, or ÷ symbols before working each problem.

- When using a periodic table in science, have students name the element and trace the symbol before copying it.

- When working equality and inequality problems in math, have students say and trace the =, >, and < symbols before working each problem.

- When revising a piece of writing which has been edited by the teacher or another student using editing marks, say and trace each mark before making the revision.

98

| C21 | **Constellation Cylinders** | Standards: 1, 2, 3, 9 |

Students can use simple materials to do this activity to learn the names of specific constellations and associate the shapes of constellations with their written and spoken names. Follow these steps:

1. Have each student cover a long cylinder can, such as a potato chip can, with black construction paper.

2. Provide each student with a white circle of paper that fits over the end of the can. Punch holes in the white paper that represent the stars in a particular constellation. Have students use the white paper as a pattern and punch holes in the closed end of the can.

3. Ask each student to use florescent, puffy paint to write the name of their constellation on the outside of the can. Have them also place dots in a pattern that represents the stars.

4. Have students hold their cylinders toward the light and look through them. Have them observe the star pattern of their constellations as they say the constellation's name and trace the shape in the air or on a tabletop.

5. Darken the room. Have students trace the painted fluorescent name on the cylinder as they say it. Have them trace the pattern and say it again.

6. Connect this activity with literature by having students read mythology. Have them share the stories that go along with each constellation as well as discuss the genre of mythology and ancient cultures.

| C22 | **Telling Time** | Standards: 3, 4 |

Use a multisensory approach to teach telling time by having your students make their own clocks. Follow these steps:

1. Write the numerals for the hours around the inside circle of a paper plate for each student. Then write the numerals for minutes in five-minute increments around the outside. Have students trace the numerals with bold marker as they say them.

2. Let students use glue to mark the hours with a straight line across the hour numerals.

3. Have students use glue to make dots for the minutes as they count aloud.

4. Let students put a line of glue on the front of two construction paper clock hands to provide texture. Then they can attach the hour and minute hands to the clock with brads.

5. Use the clocks for diverse time activities, such as these:
   a. Hold up a card with a time written out and have students say the time.
   b. Have students touch/count aloud the hours on the clock and move the hour hand to the indicated position.
   c. Have students touch/count aloud the minute dots and move the minute hand to the indicated position.
   d. Have students say the time aloud once more as they trace the clock hands.

To make telling time meaningful, ask the class to name and show times that correspond with daily activities such as lunch, recess, and computer lab. Ask individual students to name and show times for their own special activities, such as soccer practice, dance rehearsal, or study group. To integrate more reading and writing, have students create timelines or short stories that describe their daily routines and important times.

C23	**Sidewalk Maps**	Standards: 1, 2, 3, 7, 9, 10

Students can profit when maps of geographical locations are drawn with chalk, or even better — painted, on large sidewalks or other concrete surfaces. After you've drawn the map, ask students geography questions about the location and have them demonstrate their answers by moving their bodies to the appropriate spot. For example, draw a map of the students' home state with major cities, familiar towns, large bodies of water, and major highways on an outdoor concrete basketball court. Ask questions such as, "Where is your hometown? What body of water connects our state to the ocean?" and "What would be the shortest route to drive from our capitol to your town?" Have students answer the questions by moving to the correct spot on the map and stating their answers.

You can draw large maps of the nations or regions of the world in order to enhance learning. As students read literature in these settings or research distant places in social studies, have them find the specific locations on the large map. They can also add their own drawings to the map to depict characteristics of the land (crops, weather, terrain) and people (languages, dialects, customs) of the geographic regions. Bilingual students with roots in other countries can place special markings on their homelands.

C24	**Domino Addition Facts**	Standards: 3, 4

Teachers use dots on dominoes to teach basic addition facts. The dots visually represent numbers which can be added together. Follow these steps for each addition fact you want students to learn:

1. On a large card, trace a domino lengthwise and color the dots to illustrate an addition fact. Directly beside the domino, write a vertical addition problem with blanks where the numerals go. Laminate.

2. Provide students with several dominoes and have them find the real corresponding domino and lay it on the domino drawing to illustrate the problem. They can run their fingers over the domino to actually count the dots.

3. Ask students to write the correct numerals in the problem with an erasable marker. Be sure that they state the fact as they write it. (In the example on the previous page, they would write 2 + 3 = 5.)

4. If desired, you can also write a horizontal number sentence for students to complete on the card; however, keep in mind that having two number sentences on a card can confuse some students.

5. After students master the simplest facts, place two dominoes beside one another other to create more addition problems. Their resulting problems would add 4 numbers together as shown in the illustration.

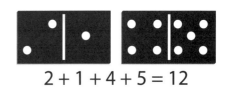

$$2 + 1 + 4 + 5 = 12$$

| C25 | **Place Charades** | Standards: 1, 3, 4, 5, 6, 7, 8, 9, 10, 11 |

Place Charades is a multisensory game that helps students become familiar with geographical locations. Here are the simple steps for this activity:

1. Before class begins, write names of local, state, or national geographical locations on one side of large note cards.

2. Divide students into groups, and give each group a card. (Tell the groups not to reveal the names of their locations to other groups.) Have each group research the location written on their card in their textbooks and encyclopedias, as well as on the Internet.

3. After each group has researched its location, direct the group to do the following:
   a. Prepare a written description of the assigned location without mentioning the name. (Encourage students to make the description vivid by using adjectives, adverbs, and other rich language.)
   b. Draw a map showing the location.
   c. Practice imitating sounds that go with the location (including animals of the area and the language or dialect spoken, if possible).
   d. Sketch pictures of daily life in the location.
   e. As an option, prepare a scent board containing scents associated with the location (put fragrances on tissue and glue the tissue to a small poster).
   f. Prepare a role-play of something that happens in that location.

4. Have each group present its location to the class, beginning with the least obvious multisensory clue. Let other groups guess the location.

Bilingual students will enjoy being in a group that represents their native land. They can be the experts and share their language and experiences.

| C26 | **Multisensory Geometry** | Standard: 4 |

Using multisensory activities can help students learn and like geometry. Try these ideas:

- Provide three-dimensional shapes that students can see, feel, describe, draw, and model.

- Provide rope that students can manipulate to make lines, angles, and shapes.

- Cut two strips of cardboard and connect them with a brad. Let students move the two strips into various angles as they orally state what they are representing.

- Have students glue colored pipe cleaners on construction paper to make angles and shapes, as well as to show geometric relationships. Later, they can trace the figures as they study them.

- Make sure that students are describing and discussing geometric concepts with each other as they learn. Having to put their ideas into words will help them clarify their thinking and help you identify misunderstandings.

| C27 | **Dramatizing Processes** | Standards: 3, 11 |

Math, science, social studies, and other content area subjects often have processes that students must understand and apply. Acting out these processes can help students remember. Provide or have students develop simple props and scripts for their dramatizations. Here are some topics that students can act out for the class:

- *Math:* addition and subtraction algorithms
- *English:* formation of contractions or compound words
- *Reading:* finding words in the dictionary
- *Social Studies:* a timeline of events
- *Health:* the food pyramid (using students to represent food groups)

| C28 | **Foreign Language Study** | Standards: 1, 3, 6, 9, 10 |

Learning foreign languages is problematic for many students with language-processing disabilities. Often they experience the same difficulties with a second language that they experience with their first one. Anxiety or a lack of time and resources can compound problems. If English is a second language for students, new foreign languages are especially difficult if students have not mastered English.

When these students are learning foreign languages, it is critical that they receive explicit, systematic instruction presented in a multisensory manner. Numerous activities in this book can be applied to foreign language instruction and study. Audiotapes and computer software tutorials also allow students extensive individual practice with language skills.

102

You will need to help students set realistic goals, break them into manageable chunks, and plan ways to achieve them. Realize that more time and effort are needed for these students to meet their goals. Give them opportunities to learn about the cultures and geography of countries in which the language is spoken and encourage them to use the new language in authentic contexts. Often students become proficient in reading and writing the new language but have problems with speaking it, or vice versa.

Some students satisfy foreign language curriculum requirements by taking Latin because it is a written, rather than a spoken language and doesn't require students to struggle to pronounce difficult words. Others take a computer language or sign language to meet foreign language requirements at their schools.

C29 | Pegboard Graphing   Standards: 4, 11

Graphing can easily be made multisensory with pegboards and pegs or golf tees. Follow these steps:

1. Buy a piece of pegboard and cut a manageable piece of it. (If students will work in groups, cut a large pegboard. If they will be working individually, cut smaller pegboards.)

2. Draw a Y axis and an X axis on the pegboard with a dark marker.

3. Have students show ordered pairs by placing pegs in the appropriate holes as they state the pairs aloud.

4. Students often like to work in partnerships with one student calling out the ordered pair and the other student placing the pegs. They then check each other's work.

5. Older students can work equations to calculate slopes of lines and use graphing calculators to check their work. Teams of students can turn this into a game with each team taking a turn with calculations and graphing.

6. Motivate students by letting them use colored yarn to connect points to make a picture.

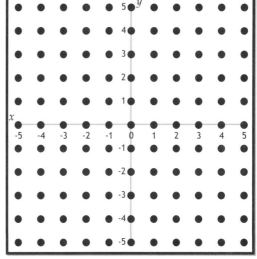

| C30 | **Reading Math Word Problems** | Standard: 3 |

Even students who learn math concepts and skills easily can have difficulties reading and solving math word problems. It is a good idea to help students begin by identifying the parts in word problems. Most problems include the following:

- *Setting* (background of the problem)
- *Facts* (information needed to solve the problem)
- *Question* (what you need to find out)

Some problems will also have:

- *Distractors* (extra information that is not needed to solve the problem)

Write a simple word problem on a poster and identify the parts using a different color or different types of markings for each part. Discuss the parts with your students and use many examples to make the connections more permanent.

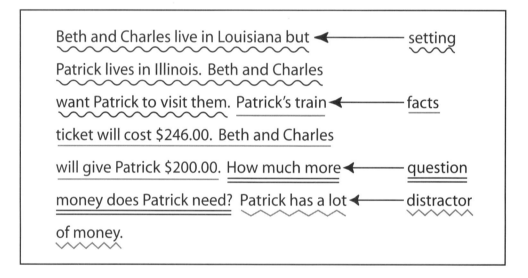

Later, as students read math word problems independently, have them code the different parts as they read them aloud. Then they can focus on the facts and the question to solve the problem quickly and correctly.

| C31 | **Tests** | Standards: 3, 4, 8 |

Students can know content area material very well but fail tests in content areas because of language problems. Be sure to give them the extra assistance they need to communicate what they know. Here are some ideas to make testing days more successful:

- Provide a relaxed atmosphere that alleviates test anxiety.

- Read test directions aloud as students follow along. Have them highlight important words or phrases, such as *circle*, *give two reasons*, or *show your work*.

- Monitor students as they work through a few examples.

- Let students tape record oral directions to listen to them again as needed.

- If students cannot read the test items, read the items to them. Often a parent volunteer can help with this. Make sure that no one accidentally gives hints.

- If students cannot write their answers, let them dictate their answers to you or a volunteer. Make sure that no one indicates correctness of answers through words, facial expressions, or gestures. Students can also dictate their answers into a tape recorder.

- Allow students to write directly on the test rather than an answer sheet, whenever possible.

- If a standardized test requires a bubble sheet, have students practice filling in bubbles and staying on the right line before test time.

- Do not penalize for spelling on tests in content areas other than spelling. When you notice important spelling errors, make a note of them for later instruction.

- Make tests *test-taker friendly*:
    - ✔ Use large, easy-to-read print.
    - ✔ Use a variety of test items (objective, essay).
    - ✔ Group items according to type (multiple choice, true/false).
    - ✔ Group the items into brief sections (two sections of five completion items, rather than one section of ten items).

- Provide ample time. Have more than one testing session if needed.

- Allow a student to take a test in another room if distraction is a problem.

- Allow students to demonstrate learning through performance-based assessments (which are usually multisensory). Examples include learning lines, posters, demonstrations, experiments, simulations, role-plays, artwork, computer presentations, and bulletin boards.

Name _____ Date _____

1. My Goal: _____

_____

_____

2. Beginning date: _____

   Steps to accomplish my goal:

   a. _____

   _____

   b. _____

   _____

   c. _____

   _____

3. Ending Date: _____

   Did I accomplish my goal? Explain. _____

   _____

   _____

4. Future Plans: _____

   _____

   _____

   _____

Reading Assignments

Date	Pages	Finished	Reward

7 Social Skills

Many professionals and most laypersons would probably describe a learning disability as "a problem with reading, writing, or math." Difficulties with social development or social interactions may not be cited or even recognized as a characteristic of the disability; however, social skills may ultimately determine an individual's academic and vocational success.

Research and anecdotal records reveal that individuals with learning disabilities demonstrate inappropriate and challenging behaviors more frequently and extremely than do their nondisabled peers. This is particularly true for individuals who are learning disabled and have attention deficit disorder (ADD) and attention deficit with hyperactivity disorder (ADHD).

You may be wondering why we included a chapter on social skills in a language arts book. We have some good reasons. Individual characteristics, academic failure, and poorly developed or inadequate language skills partially explain why many students with learning disabilities have emotional problems (low self-esteem, anxiety, depression), as well as conduct problems (outburst, impatience, delinquency), as well as receive differential treatment from their teachers and parents, including rejection and ridicule.

The activities in this chapter are designed to increase students' social skills development and reinforce appropriate behaviors. Inappropriate or challenging behaviors should be ignored except when they pose a risk for causing injury to the student or others. Teachers and parents should consult with school counselors, psychologists, and other appropriate health care providers for specific recommendations. There are children with learning disabilities who are also emotionally disturbed, and these children may need intensive, individualized psychological or medical intervention. Some resources where you can find information about social skills are included in this chapter.

Goals

- To promote development of social skills
- To use language appropriately in social situations
- To inventory social behaviors for appropriateness
- To provide alternatives for challenging behaviors
- To build an appreciation and understanding of self and others
- To provide informational resources to support teachers, parents, and students

S1	## Inventory of Social Competency	Standards: 9, 12

Are you aware of a student's social competency? Do you know how frequently a behavior occurs? Does the frequency or intensity of the behavior vary with the context? Do poor language skills contribute to the conduct problem?

Complete the **Inventory of Social Competency** on page 119 by checking the column that indicates the frequency of the directly observed or reported behaviors. Both positive and negative behaviors have been purposefully included. Target behaviors for extinction that most frequently appear and most negatively impact the student's overall development and performance. Reinforce behaviors that are appropriate and encourage social competency.

You might have the student or peers complete the inventory. In that case, it is recommended that you delete the title from the student's page to diminish any feelings of social inadequacy.

S2	## Positive Image	Standards: 9, 12

A positive self image is critical to academic success. This activity encourages students to appreciate themselves. Have students work in pairs, and have one student lay on a large sheet of butcher paper while his partner traces the outline of his body. Then have them switch places and repeat the activity. Encourage students to use crayons, markers, or paint to draw in their own facial features and clothes. You can provide materials such as yarn for hair, buttons for eyes, or material for clothing for the students to paste onto their outlines to individualize their images. Next, have students cut out their figures. Post the figures around the room and tell students, "Now let's take some time to describe ourselves." Model positive descriptions about body images, such as "I have big blue eyes and curly brown hair." Ask students to look at their outlines and describe themselves in similar, positive ways.

S3	## Say Something Nice	Standards: 9, 12

Students often use descriptors such as *stupid, fat, smelly,* and *stuck up* to label other students in their class. You can involve the whole class in limiting such inappropriate labels and improving self-concept by giving each student a copy of the class list. Ask each student to write descriptive, complimentary words next to every name on the list. You might begin by displaying a word bank with positive descriptors on an overhead or chalkboard. Encourage students to brainstorm descriptors to add to the word bank.

After students have finished adding descriptors for each name, collect the lists and review all of the descriptors for each student. Create a master list of appropriate descriptors and post them in the classroom. You might tape the descriptors for each student on that student's desk as a reminder of positive qualities, or they can be posted next to the student's cutout image that was created in activity **S2**. This activity will help students develop an understanding of and respect for students who speak different languages and who are from different cultures, ethnic groups, and geographic regions. Here are some examples of descriptors you might lead your students to include:

runs fast	is friendly
plays the trumpet	shares with others
has pretty handwriting	is good in math
is polite	works hard
is a good basketball player	can keep a secret

S4 — People Puzzle
Standards: 7, 9, 12

You can use a People Puzzle to heighten your students' sensitivity to diversity. Have your students use the outlined images they made in activity **S2**, and cut them into their major body parts (arms, legs, body, head). Then have students work with others to use all their parts to assemble new "people" using body parts from each other's figures. You can put students of different cultural and linguistic background in the same group to see how different their new creations look from their originals. Help students research and talk about the similarities and differences among all people including their languages, celebrations, customs, and rituals.

S5 — Role-Playing
Standards: 8, 12

Students with language and learning disabilities may have difficulty interpreting social situations and the appropriateness of their own social interactions. You can use role-playing to teach appropriate social behaviors. Here are some suggestions for activities you can have your students role-play:

- Introducing a friend to a stranger
- Requesting help from a teacher
- Apologizing for hurting a friend's feelings
- How to stop an argument and still "save face"
- Asking a parent for permission to visit a friend's house
- Taking a telephone message
- Requesting information over the phone

It is often beneficial to videotape a student's role-play attempt and critique the actions as you watch it together. You should be aware that a student may be embarrassed or humiliated if his session is critiqued by a group of peers; therefore, you may want to conduct individual review sessions to discuss the student's appropriate or inappropriate behaviors.

| S6 | **Social Stories** | Standards: 1, 4, 12 |

Social stories teach social skills by placing students into situations that require social responses. The two most common types of social stories are as follows:

- **Descriptive:** Describe what people do in social situations (describe social setting and step-by-step directions for completing an activity or task).

- **Directive:** Direct a person to an appropriate desired response (state the desired behavior in positive terms).

You can develop a story that prepares students for a new situation, to teach more appropriate social interactions, or to discuss alternative behaviors. Use flannel board pictures to depict situations and people, and have students write their responses to the social situations that are presented. Here are some topics for story development:

- Why sometimes you don't get an answer from others
- Asking questions you know the answer to
- Touching other's property
- Leaving an enjoyable activity
- "Tuning in" to people
- Predicting what's going to happen later
- Calling out whenever you want to talk to someone
- Looking at people and stopping what you're doing when they are talking
- Stopping an activity when told to
- Interrupting when others are talking or busy doing something
- Listening the first time someone tells you something
- Doing your best the first time and every time

| S7 | **Journaling** | Standards: 4, 5, 11, 12 |

Journal writing provides students with a mechanism for expression when they have difficulty verbally expressing their feelings. People are often reluctant to talk about their problems, even with a friend or family member, because they are afraid the other person may think less of them. A journal is a private way for students to explore their thoughts and feelings.

A simple notebook can serve as a journal. Have students decorate the cover of their journals to display their individuality. Set aside a regularly scheduled time each day for journal writing. You can also encourage parents to set a time at home for journaling. Encourage students to write, draw, or paint in their journals. Students' journal entries should be private, and they should not be read by anyone, unless the student gives permission to do so.

S8	**Think Out Loud**	Standards: 4, 12

Students can learn to deal with impulsive behavior if they are given time to slow down before they respond. Provide students with a hypothetical problem and have them verbalize the steps they would use to work through a problem. You might say, "Think out loud about what you should do and tell me the steps you are going to use." By taking the time to reason through the situation and verbalize their thoughts and feelings, students learn how to solve their problems with less impulsivity. Students are much more likely to use this metacognitive approach the next time they encounter a similar situation.

S9	**My Buddy**	Standards: 4, 6, 9, 10, 12

Students with learning disabilities can have problems building and keeping friendships. Having students work in pairs on assignments will help them learn to cooperate, compromise, and appreciate each other's abilities. Tolerance for others, if not friendships, may also be fostered during these interactions. Working in pairs is especially good for students to develop an understanding of and respect for students who are learning English as a second language or who are from different cultures.

Pair students with complimentary skills to work together on assignments or projects. For example, two students who have read the same book can work together on one book report. One student who likes to draw can illustrate the cover and pages of the report, and the other student who likes to type and use the computer can type the report.

S10	**Autobiography**	Standards: 5, 6, 7, 8, 11

Students can learn interesting things about themselves and other students through autobiographies. Have students collect information about themselves (names of family members, their country of origin, family crest) and create an electronic or paper portfolio. Students might use software graphic organizers to design their family trees; presentation software with voice overlays to narrate their family's story; and digital cameras to take pictures of immediate family members, friends, homes, interests, etc. If possible, have students develop their own web pages to display the information they collected, or they can organize and display printed information in ringed binders.

| S11 | **Think Out Loud** | Standards: 4, 9, 12 |

Children adopt feelings and attitudes from others in their environment. Family members and friends may say things to them like, "You're so hard headed. Why do you always have to have it your way?" or "You're never going to graduate with grades like these." Have the students discuss how they feel when they hear these emotional messages. Write emotional messages in red pen on an overhead or on one side of a sheet of paper. Then have the students write the corresponding informational messages in green pen on the other side of the paper. Teach students to rephrase emotional messages into informational messages whenever they hear them. Here are some examples:

Emotional messages	Informational messages
You're so hard headed.	I believe in this. That's why I'm not changing my mind.
You never listen.	I listened, but I didn't understand what you wanted me to do.
You always have to have it your way.	No, but I want you to consider other options.
You look funny.	I look the way I like to look, not the way you want me to look.

| S12 | **Games** | Standards: 1, 4, 9, 10*, 12 |

Structure free time in the classroom when students can play games that teach cooperation, critical thinking, reading, good gamesmanship, and communication skills, such as sequencing, following directions, asking a question, and reading directions. Games can be traditional board or card games with two or more players, or software and CD games with multiple players and controllers. The entire class can play some games when students are divided into teams. Be sure the teams include students with varying abilities, interests, and ethnic groups. Here are some examples of appropriate games, including the publisher's name, and recommended age groups:

- *Math and Music* (Wildridge) 8 years and up
- *Great States Board Game* (International Playthings) 7 years and up
- *Cranium* (Cranium) 12 years and up
- *Moneywise Kids* (Aristoplay) 7 years and up
- *Deluxe Scrabble* (Milton Bradley) 8 years and up
- *Jeopardy* (Parker Brothers) 8 years and up
- *The Weakest Link* (Hasbro) 12 years and up
- *Word Thief* (Faby Game Word) 8 years and up
- *Who Wants to Be a Millionaire* Board Game or CD (Pressman Toys) 12 years and up
- *The Ellis Island Experience* (South Peak Interactive) 11 years to adult*
- *Talking Walls* (Edmark) 8 to 14 years*

| S13 | **What Ifs?** | **Standards: 4, 5, 9, 12** |

Parents and educators often use the phrase "What if?" as a way of having children reflect on their behavior. We often say, "What if someone did that to you?" or "What if everyone felt that way?"

You can use "What Ifs?" to teach alternative solutions to situations and increase the students' appreciation for consequences. Write "What If?" questions on individual index cards. Place the cards in a paper bag. Have individual students reach into the bag and pull out a card. Have the student read the card aloud and provide a solution. Ask the class to discuss alternative solutions and consequences of the solutions. Here are some examples of questions you might use:

- What if a younger child hit you?
- What if your friend _____? (did something inappropriate or against the rules)
- What if I cried every time you told me I couldn't do something?
- What if I broke your favorite toy and didn't tell you?
- What if you didn't speak English and no one helped you at school?

As a variation for the verbal activity, pose specific "What If?" questions to the class and have students write their solutions. You might choose specific topics to highlight a problem that frequently occurs for more than one student or for a problem that affects the majority of students in the class. Have students read their solutions to the questions and discuss their suggestions.

| S14 | **Asking for Help** | **Standards: 4, 5, 9, 12** |

Students often develop behavior problems because they have difficulty asking for help. We often ask, "Does anyone have any questions?" and students shake their heads in negation. We also ask, "Does everyone understand?" and students either respond, "Yes" or nod their heads in affirmation. Yet, in a one-on-one situation, students are more apt to admit to their teachers that they don't understand a concept or an assignment. Students of all ages and at every grade level have great difficulty asking for help. How can students ask for help without looking incompetent in front of their peers? How can they let the teacher know they don't understand without having others laugh at them? That is the quandary many students face.

Nonverbal group responses where no one else knows each other's answers provide students with a sense of security. You can use eraser boards for group answers. Students can write the answer to a question on their eraser boards and on signal, hold up their boards in unison. Scan the boards to determine which students' answers are correct or incorrect. Depending on the number of correct and incorrect answers, you can continue teaching, re-teach the information to the class, or note students who need individual attention. Similarly, you can ask, "Does anyone have any questions?" or "Does everyone understand?" and the students can write "Yes" or "No" on their eraser boards.

| S15 | **Rant 'n' Rave Box** | Standards: 4, 5, 12 |

Sometimes we all want to tell someone how angry we are or how much we appreciate something special someone did for us, but we don't have the words to express our feelings. Have students create a classroom "Rant 'N Rave" box where students can write things on index cards they want to rant about and things they wanted to rave about.

Have students anonymously submit their cards any time of the day. Periodically empty the box and look over the cards. Lead class discussions to talk about ideas that can be implemented, or things that can be omitted or revised. You can also intervene when students rant about personal or interpersonal problems.

| S16 | **Past and Present** | Standards: 4, 9, 12 |

Students interact and develop social skills when they are familiar and comfortable with those in their surroundings. Students can learn each other's names and interests by comparing pictures from the past with the present. Collect baby pictures of the students in the class and have students glue or tape their pictures onto 8.5" x 11" pieces of construction paper. Have each student write a caption under the baby picture describing current interests, ambitions, etc. Randomly distribute the captioned pictures to the students in the class and have them guess which classmate's baby picture they are holding. Encourage students to discuss with one another how they have changed over the years.

Resources

Appalachia Educational Laboratory. (n.d.). Preventing antisocial behavior in disabled and at-risk students. Retrieved January 19, 2002, from http://www.ldonline.org/ld_indepth/ add_adhd/ael_behavior.html

Currie, P., & Wadlington, E. (2000). *The source for learning disabilities.* East Moline, Il.: LinguiSystems.

DeGeorge, K. L. (1998, January) Friendship and stories: using children's literature to teach friendship skills to children with learning disabilities. *Intervention in school and clinic, 33* (3) 157-162. Retrieved January 19, 2002, from http://www.ldonline.org/ ld_indepth/teaching_techniques/childlit_socskills.html

Step-by-step methods for teaching friendship skills and a listing of books about making friends.

Lavoie, R. (1994). *Social competence and the child with learning disabilities.* Retrieved January 19, 2002, from http://www.ldonline.org/ld_indepth/social_skills/lavoie_quest.html

Lyons, J. (1998). *Gather stars for your children: songs to enhance social skills and to foster a welcoming attitude.* Retrieved on January 19, 2002, from http://www.bitlink.com/jeannelyons/

RGK Foundation. (2001, October 1). Dyslexia and English as a second language (including blingualism): issues, research, diagnosis, instruction, and future directions. Video Webcast from http://www.connectlive.com/events/dyslexia/

Internet Website Resources

ERIC Clearinghouse on Disabilities and Gifted Education
    Selected Internet Resources for Learning Disabilities
    http://wricec.org/faq/ldsped-x.html

Horn-Hoffer, C. Social Stories for AS and Autistic Children
    http://members.tripod.com/gcanik/id38.htm

LD OnLine
    Bulletin Boards for Social Skills
    http://forums.weta.org/ldonline/phorum/list.php?f=11

Learning Potentials
    Programs to Improve Children's Self-esteem
    Self-help tapes for children and parents
    http://www.learningpotentials.com

References

ADDinSchool.com. (n.d.). *Suggestions for setting up the classroom to maximize the performance of children with ADD and ADHD.* Retrieved January 19, 2002, from http://ww.addinschool.com/elementary/roomsetup.htm

Bos, C. S., & Vaughn, S. (1988). *Strategies for teaching students with learning and behavior problems.* Boston: Allyn & Bacon.

Polloway, E. A., Patton, J. R., Payne, J. S., & Payne, R. A. (1989). *Strategies for teaching learners with special needs.* Columbus, OH: Merrill.

Lavoie, R. (1994). *Social competence and the child with learning disabilities.* Retrieved January 19, 2002, from http://www.ldonline.org/ld_indepth/social_skills/lavoie_quest.html

Inventory of Social Competency

Check (✔) the column that indicates the frequency with which the behavior occurs.

Name:		Date:		
Characteristic	**Seldom**	**Frequently**	**Always**	
1. chooses unacceptable behavior in social situations				
2. solves social problems without assistance				
3. changes language and behavior to fit social situation				
4. predicts consequences of behavior				
5. adjusts to the characteristics of listeners in discussions or conversation				
6. is rejected or isolated by classmates or peers				
7. adapts to new social situations				
8. tolerates frustration and failure				
9. uses less mature expressive language				
10. misunderstands what he hears or reads				
11. uses words rather than physical actions to solve problems				
12. demonstrates self control				
13. responds to strong incentives				
14. distracted				
15. learns from previous mistakes				
16. knows when to demonstrate appropriate behaviors				
17. interrupts				
18. accepts responsibility for actions				
19. recognizes school or family routines				
20. self-regulates emotions—especially temper				
21. participates in extracurricular activities				
22. recognizes and interprets social cues				
23. impatient				
24. overreacts				
25. demonstrates problem-solving skills				
26. displays positive self-esteem				
27. is organized				

8 Home Activities

Language and emergent literacy skills begin to develop before children enter preschool. Here are some ways those skills begin to emerge:

- Children develop an understanding and respect for the diversity of cultures and languages by listening to stories others read to them.

- Expressive language skills develop as children retell or create their own stories.

- Literacy emerges as young children "read" stories by pointing to and describing pictures in books or magazines and as they "write" words and sentences to tell about themselves or to label objects in their environment.

As you can see, parents and early childhood educators play a critical role in laying the foundation for literacy development.

Parents and early interventionists can be powerful advocates for children with disabilities, but they must recognize and execute their roles and responsibilities as members of the child's multidisciplinary team. A multidisciplinary team includes many different people, and the composition of the team is dictated by the student's profile. The team is minimally composed of the student, the parents, and the regular and special education teachers; however, other professionals may be involved, including a psychologist, medical personnel, and a speech-language pathologist.

The Individuals with Disabilities Education Act (IDEA) of 1997 highlighted the importance of parental involvement in the educational process for children with disabilities by including parents in all stages of the identification and assessment procedures and in the development of educational plans. IDEA additionally provided parents with the right to have input during the pre-referral and eligibility meetings and to help plan positive behavioral interventions for their child.

Educators and support personnel who work with children with learning disabilities must collaborate with parents in order to better serve students. Consistent and effective communication must take place among all team members. Educators need to provide parents with current and accurate information about the disorder and the educational process, including the parents' due process rights. Parents should also be introduced to effective intervention methods, such as multisensory teaching techniques and materials. Parents should tell educators about their child's strengths and weaknesses, as well as any medical needs. Collaboration is improved when information is freely and openly exchanged, and it increases the likelihood that sound educational decisions will be made and implemented. This chapter emphasizes the role parents and early interventionists play in the development of language and literacy. Goals and activities are provided for the various members of the child's multidisciplinary team.

Goals

- To promote language and literacy in the home
- To fully participate in the student's educational process
- To be knowledgeable about the student's disorder
- To be knowledgeable about various educational and medical interventions
- To openly communicate with all team members
- To analyze tasks to solve issues
- To select appropriate solutions to tasks and develop an intervention plan
- To follow through with the intervention plan
- To evaluate the effectiveness of the intervention plan
- To make appropriate modifications to the intervention plan

| H1 | **Model Literacy** | Standards: 2, 5, 9, 10, 11, 12 |

Children who are exposed to literature in the home are much more likely to develop literacy skills than children who are reared in homes that do not have reading and writing materials. Parents can promote their child's literacy development by modeling reading and writing.

Literature can create a bridge between a child's life experiences and academic learning, and multicultural literature reflects cultural diversity within the community and classroom. Families can read a wide range of literature from many different authors and that are written in a child's primary or native language, and parents can read or translate the story into English. Speakers of different dialects can choose stories written in their own dialect, as well as stories written in Standard English.

Parents can model literacy by doing the following:
- Making various types of literature and writing instruments in the home accessible to the child
- Collecting reading materials that the child selects and enjoys
- Regularly reading to the child from various types of literature (big picture books, storybooks with sing-a-long or read-a-long tapes)
- Pointing to pictures and words in printed text as they orally read
- Providing or asking the child for the English equivalent for words written in the primary or native language
- Pausing to ask the child questions about a story or to predict what might happen next
- Writing for different purposes with the child's participation (grocery lists, to-do lists, sending virtual greeting cards on the Internet to family and friends)

| H2 | **Chalk Games** | Standards: 3, 5, 12 |

Children enjoy playing games, especially those that require large muscle movements. You can use colored sidewalk chalk to promote literacy development and specific reading skills.

Here are some suggestions for chalk games for young children who are developing emergent literacy:
- Write the child's name in a light-colored chalk and have the child trace inside the letters with a dark-colored chalk.
- Play number games, such as hopscotch, and have the participants name the numbers as they play. The child can trace or connect-the-dots to write the numbers prior to beginning the game.

- Draw shapes or figures, such as the ones on the right (rectangle, bird), and have the child guess the name of each. Have the child write the first letter of the name of the shape or figure under each figure. Have the child say the letter's name and tell you its sound.

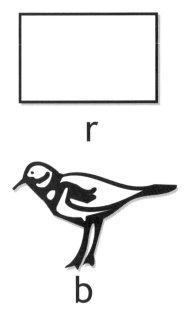

Here are some chalk games you can play with older, more skilled students:

- Draw a nine-box square on the sidewalk. Write a spelling word, vocabulary word, or a word that contains a specific grammatical rule (words that end in *x*, *sh*, *ch* that are pluralized by adding -*es*) in each box. Use different-colored chalk to highlight components of the words. One child throws a beanbag onto a square and reads the word, uses it in a sentence, spells the word, etc.
- Play hangman or blackout using spelling or vocabulary words.

H3	**Team Building**	Standards: 3, 4, 8, 11, 12

Education has become more family-centered — a concept that shifts the focus of decision-making from educators to family members (Robinson, 1997). The National PTA worked diligently to obtain parental involvement as one of the eight National Education Goals: "Every school will promote partnerships that will increase parental involvement and participation in promoting the social, emotional and academic growth of children" (National PTA, 2001).

The importance of parent/family involvement is especially true for children with disabilities. Parents should collaborate with educators and support personnel to build family and professional teams. Team members can ask themselves the following questions to determine how well their team operates:

- Are all team members readily accessible to one another?
- Do team members frequently communicate with one another?
- Are appropriate team members present at all meetings?
- Are team members comfortable interacting with one another?
- Are participants acknowledged for their input and is their input valued?
- Do team members provide accurate and meaningful information?
- Are professional reports and other forms of written communication jargon-free and understandable to nonprofessionals?

Teams can conduct inventories of its members to determine the most effective and efficient ways to communicate with one another. The **Communication Questionnaire** on page 136 may help your team establish effective lines of communication.

| H4 | **Listen, Read, and Ask Questions** | **Standards: 1, 7, 8, 12** |

Parents obtain valuable information about their child's disability and the educational process from the multidisciplinary team, but parents and students have to take on the responsibility to educate themselves about learning disabilities. There are many different viewpoints about the etiology of learning disabilities, about the type and manner of assessment, and about the effectiveness of intervention techniques. Information about learning disabilities can be found in books and journals, as well as from other parents and people who post messages to discussion boards and talk in chat rooms on the Internet, informative videos, support groups, and at professional conferences. Students and parents have to be knowledgeable about a topic before they can ask the right questions and make the best decisions for themselves or for their child.

The following sources can provide helpful information about learning disabilities:

- Families and Advocates for Partnership in Education (FAPE)
  PACER Center
  8161 Normandale Blvd.
  Minneapolis, MN 55437
  888-248-0822
  http://www.fape.org/

- Hall, S.L., & Moats, L. C. (1999). *Straight talk about reading: How parents can make a difference during the early years.* New York: NTC Publishing Group.

- The Council for Exceptional Children (CEC)
  1920 Association Drive
  Reston, VA 22091-1589
  800-328-0272
  http://www.cec.sped.org/

- National PTA
  330 N. Wabash Ave., Suite 2100
  Chicago, IL 60611-3690
  (312) 6706782 (voice)
  (312) 670-6783 (FAX)
  Email: info@pta.org
  http://www.pta.org

- Learning Disabilities Association (LDA)
  4156 Library Road
  Pittsburgh, PA 15234-1349
  (412) 341-1515 (voice)
  (412) 344-0224 (FAX)
  http://www.ldanatl.org/

H5	**Use Positive Reinforcers**	Standard: 8

Reinforcing a behavior increases the likelihood that it will continue or increase in frequency. Reinforcement is either positive or negative. Positive reinforcement is *given* on the condition that the individual demonstrates a desired behavior. As a result, reinforcers or rewards are given to individuals when they demonstrate a desired behavior. "The child earns 15 minutes of free time for demonstrating appropriate classroom behaviors" is a typical reward. Negative reinforcement is when an unpleasant or unwanted condition is *removed* when the individual demonstrates a desired behavior (Roth & Worthington, 1997). Most learning theorists and child developmental specialists believe that positive reinforcement should be implemented whenever possible.

The two basic types of reinforcers are called *primary* and *secondary*. Primary reinforcers are those items or conditions that have a positive effect on the person's physiology, such as food. Primary reinforcers are often used with young children, and they are used to establish a new behavior. Secondary reinforcers are items or conditions that the individual identifies as rewarding. Examples include playing a certain game or watching a favorite TV show. Both types of reinforcers have to be selected on a person-by-person basis because a reward for one person isn't necessarily a reinforcer for another. Verbal reinforcers can be very powerful, yet they may lack potency for students with learning disabilities because of their receptive language limitations.

Parents and educators have to identify effective reinforcers for each child. A common way to identify reinforcers is to have the child complete an interest inventory or questionnaire, such as the **Reinforcer Inventory** on page 137. Parents of young children or early interventionists can complete the questionnaire based on their knowledge of and interactions with the children.

Note: Do not include an activity as a reward if you are not willing or able to provide it.

Here are some areas you might consider for rewards:
- Favorite foods
  Caution: Consider the food's nutritional value and any medical condition, such as diabetes or allergies, that might limit certain foods from a child's diet.

- Favorite activities
  ✔ Indoor and outdoor activities
  ✔ Solitary or group activities

- Need for feedback about quality of performance
  ✔ Immediate vs. delayed feedback

H6	**Multisensory Directions**	Standards: 3, 4

Individuals with learning disabilities often have difficulty following multi-step directions. They have difficulty holding information in working memory because of inadequate auditory processing skills, attention, language concepts, or vocabulary. Remember the following when giving directions:

- Limit the number of directions given at one time.

- Have the child reverbalize the directions prior to executing them.

- Gesture in the direction of key objects or places noted in the direction.
  "Go to the laundry room (point to the direction of the laundry room) and put your tennis shoes (hold them up for the child to see) on top of the dryer."

- Describe the key object's function to aid vocabulary comprehension.
  *"Put it next to the **air compressor** — the thing Daddy uses to put air in your bike tires."*

- Use ordinal numbers (first, second, third) to help the student sequence the order in which the direction should be executed.
  *"**First**, put your lunch bag away. **Second**, take your school bag into your room. **Third**, take off your school clothes."*

  You can place additional emphasis on order by using gestures. Hold up **one finger** to indicate the **first** part of the instruction, **two fingers** to reflect the **second** part, and **three fingers** for the **third** part.

  Following the direction, ask the child, "How many things do you have to do?" The restatement will help the child remember the number of steps in the direction. If the child can't remember or confuses the steps, it will cue you to repeat the direction. Repeat the directions and use gestures if you didn't do so the first time.

- Vary your voice for emphasis. You can emphasize the parts of the directions or key words by pausing after each ordinal number or by slightly increasing your volume on key words.

H7	**Visualize Goals**	Standards: 3, 4

How many times have you said, "I can see it" when you are asked to recall something. You can *see* the page on which the information is written, you know if a word is spelled correctly if you *see* it written, and you can remember the color of the ink you used to write notes in the page's margins. Even though you can visualize all those things, you still can't remember the specific information.

Visualization is a technique that aids memory and recall. Information that enters through the visual pathways is often more easily stored in your memory than information that is only presented through the auditory channel. The adage "A picture is worth a thousand words" aptly applies to visualization. Encourage children to try these visualization techniques:

- Close their eyes as they listen to directions. Picture themselves doing the things required in the directions.

  For example, "Go to the reference shelf; pull the encyclopedia from the shelf that has information with E; locate information about Albert Einstein; E-i-n-s-t-e-i-n.

- Have a mental image of the completed project before beginning the project.

- Concentrate on the details of the completed project. Write down these details. The detailed notes will help organize the materials needed for the project.

- Picture yourself doing and completing the task. Visualization can reduce anxiety associated with a stressful task.

  For example, a student might say the following to prepare for an oral book report: "I can see my teacher standing in front of the class as she calls out my name. It's my turn to give my report. I see myself going to the front of the class. I see myself standing in front of my classmates. I make eye contact with my classmates as I occasionally glance down at my note cards. I finish the report and return to my desk. I was great!"

| H8 | **Tracking Charts** | **Standards: 4, 8, 12** |

Students with learning and language disabilities may become easily confused with abstract rules and consequences. For example, consider the rule, "If you are not honest, you will be punished." What exactly does honest mean? What type of punishment would you receive? Those concepts are too abstract for a concrete thinker.

A tracking chart visually displays rules, responsibilities, and rewards. It diminishes the chance for confusion and conflict, and it helps reinforce desired behaviors. Parents frequently use charts to track family responsibilities, such as weekly chores and allowances. Educators use tracking charts to visually represent many different aspects of students' educational programs, including grades, behavior, and attendance. A sample completed tracking chart is shown here.

Tasks	M	T	W	Th	Fr	S	Su	M	T	W	Th	Fr	S	Su
1. make your bed	✔	✔	✔		✔			✔	✔		✔			
2. write all assignments in assignment pad	✔	✔	✔	✔	✔			✔	✔	✔		✔		

Reward: *five checks in a row=one movie rental*
ten checks in a row=one friend can sleep over

Parents can use the blank **Tracking Chart** on page 138 to explicitly write their own rules and consequences. Place the chart prominently where all of those who are involved in the tasks can see it. Students can track their own performances to heighten their awareness about reaching their goals.

H9	**Contracts**	Standard: 12

Getting students to complete homework and do other tasks is often a source of friction for many families. Using contracts is one way to alleviated some of those problems.

Contracts are written agreements between two or more individuals. Contracts describe or list expectations of those who enter into the agreement. They include consequences or penalties for noncompliance and deadlines by which the agreement is to be completed. Specific requirements in a contract can be listed and monitored using the **Tracking Chart** on page 138 and described in activity **H8**. Families can work with school personnel to develop their child's contract. You will find a blank **Contract** on page 139. Following are two sample completed contracts. The first contract contains a consequence, and the second details a reward.

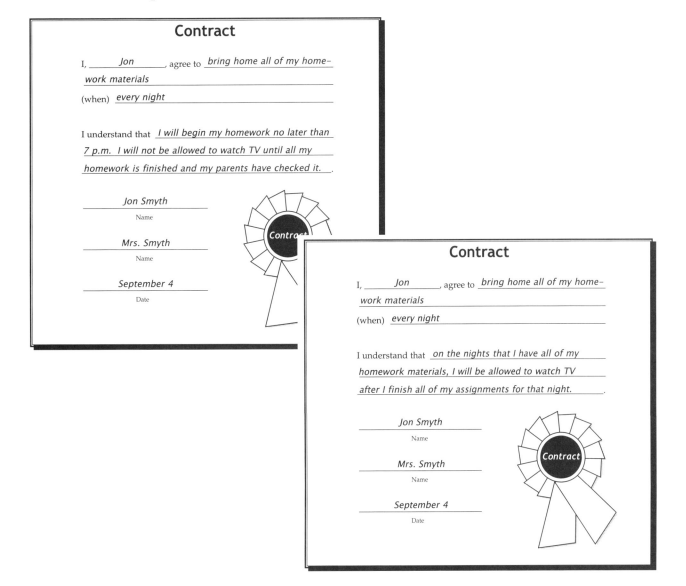

Contract

I, _____Jon_____, agree to _bring home all of my home-_
work materials
(when) _every night_

I understand that _I will begin my homework no later than_
7 p.m. I will not be allowed to watch TV until all my
homework is finished and my parents have checked it. .

_____Jon Smyth_____
Name

_____Mrs. Smyth_____
Name

_____September 4_____
Date

Contract

I, _____Jon_____, agree to _bring home all of my home-_
work materials
(when) _every night_

I understand that _on the nights that I have all of my_
homework materials, I will be allowed to watch TV
after I finish all of my assignments for that night. .

_____Jon Smyth_____
Name

_____Mrs. Smyth_____
Name

_____September 4_____
Date

| H10 | **Responsibility for Behavior** | Standards: 3, 4, 12 |

Parents and educators should carefully explain to students family or school rules and the consequences for breaking the rules. It is also important that students develop responsibility for their behavior and that they learn how to provide alternatives for their unacceptable behavior.

Parents, educators, and students should join together to develop a behavior plan that accomplishes the following (Behavior Report, 2001):

- Describes the unacceptable behavior
- Identifies which rule or rules were broken
- Outlines the consequences for breaking the rules
- Asks the student for an alternative behavior
- Outlines the consequences if the undesired behavior reoccurs

The **Individual Behavior Plan** on page 140 is a good tool for beginning to shape student behavior.

| H11 | **Family Time** | Standards: 9, 11, 12 |

You've probably heard a variation of the advice that "It's not the amount of time you spend with your child; it's the quality of the time." We often hear the catch phrase "quality time" associated with child rearing, and there is much truth to the saying. However, no one could dispute that the quality *and* quantity of time parents or care-givers spend with their child have a significant impact on the child's overall development.

Families should regularly strive to carve out uninterrupted time for themselves. Time spent together can be used to talk about family values, to make plans for upcoming outings, to watch movies, or to play games. Quality time provides parents and children with opportunities for communication as well as insight into each other's aspirations and feelings.

One parent may decide to spend time with one or more children while the other parent devotes his or her attention to a different child or children. Oftentimes, the whole family enjoys activities together. Many families have "game night" when they play board and card games together. Important language skills are required to play these games: learning and remembering the rules of the games, learning and using appropriate social skills, deciding on the best strategy to win the game, and asking questions of other players. Look at your schedule and see how you can plan to spend more quality time on a regular basis with your family.

| H12 | **Use Every Opportunity to Teach** | Standards: 4, 9, 10, 11, 12 |

People are much more likely to store and recall information when it is presented in meaningful contexts. Information may be stored in short-term memory or working memory by looking at pictures or flash cards, but these types of rote memory activities do not promote comprehension and generalization of information. Learning is optimized when information is placed in context. Teach a new concept or new word in the context in which it is needed. For example, you can teach new vocabulary and categorization skills while shopping at the grocery store. You can describe items by their category, size, color, texture, or taste. You might describe a papaya as a small, oval-shaped fruit that is red, yellow, and orange in color and smells and tastes sweet. Ask your child to name an item that fits into a category that you've named, or you name several items from the same category and have your child provide the category label.

Here is a list of routines and language concepts that take advantage of opportunities to teach:

Home
- **Cooking**
    - ✔ Tastes of food (sour, salty, sweet),
    - ✔ Smells of spices and foods (vanilla, cinnamon, onions, garlic)
    - ✔ Measurements (cooking temperatures, cooking time, weights)

Community
- **Directions and directionality** — Visualize location of stores or parks (two blocks down on the left, across the street from the school, two miles east of the interstate).
- **Services** — Discuss different types of public services and the fees for services (parking, utilities, sales tax).
- **Multicultural** — Explore the cultures, languages, and cuisine of people from different ethnic and cultural backgrounds. Taste foods from different cultures served in community restaurants. Attend different cultural activities in your community and learn about that culture's clothing, music, and art.

Environment
- Learn about the different species of animals in your region. Visit the local zoo, nature walks, or museums.
- Discuss current environmental issues as they arise. Topics may include the impact of pollution on the environment, containment of environmentally hazardous materials, depletion of the ozone, etc.

131

| H13 | **"I Spy" and "I'm Thinking About Something"** | Standards: 4, 9 |

"I Spy" and "I'm Thinking About Something" are two games that use multisensory clues to answer questions. The following questions have visual, auditory, tactile, or kinesthetic clues and you can use them during your daily activities or routines. For a different version of "I Spy" that focuses on word features, see activity **R10** on page 45.

These are games parents and children can play together. Say one clue at a time to a partner. If your partner can't identify your subject, give the second clue. Keep giving clues until your partner names the subject or you can't provide additional clues.

I Spy	I'm Thinking of Something
• I spy something gray. • I spy something that is gray and hard. • I spy something that is gray, hard, and heavy. • I spy something that is gray, hard, heavy, and it's rough. • I spy a *boulder (or stone)*. • I spy something blue. • I spy something that is blue and big. • I spy something that is blue, big, with wheels. • I spy something that is blue, big, with wheels, and it has a loud horn. • I spy an *18-wheeler*. • I spy something yellow. • I spy something yellow and furry. • I spy something yellow, furry, and soft. • I spy something yellow, furry, soft, and it purrs. • I spy a *cat*.	• I'm thinking of something heavy. • I'm thinking of something heavy and its skin is rough. • I'm thinking of something heavy, its skin is rough, and it trumpets. • I'm thinking of an *elephant*. • I'm thinking of something that tastes delicious. • I'm thinking of something that tastes delicious and it's cold. • I'm thinking of something that tastes delicious, it's cold, and it's brown and white. • I'm thinking of *chocolate-vanilla swirl yogurt (or ice cream)*. • I'm thinking of something wet. • I'm thinking of something wet that makes bubbles. • I'm thinking of something wet, that makes bubbles, and it smells like strawberries. • I'm thinking of a *strawberry bubble bath*.

Use the models above to create your own "I Spy" and "I'm Thinking of Something" games.

| H14 | **In the Mail** | Standards: 1, 3, 5, 7, 8, 12 |

Children get excited when they receive mail that is personally addressed to them. They want to open it, read it, and discuss its contents. Parents and children can collaborate to request information about tourist attractions or areas. State tourism bureaus will often send a variety of information to students who request it. Parents and older children can log on to a multitude of websites that will send information on a variety of topics and products, and sometimes even free samples of products (a search will return several sites to explore). Parents should be strongly cautioned, however, that sites offering "free" information and products often collect personal and mailing information to share with marketing companies. Parents should find out all they can about a site before submitting a name and address, and should always supervise children when visiting such sites.

| H15 | **Family Vacations and Trips** | Standards: 1, 3, 5, 7, 8, 12 |

Family discussions and planning sessions for vacations or short day trips are great opportunities for children to work on their language, reading, and writing skills. Children can search the Internet for maps that show routes and distances to possible vacation or trip sites. Have children request information online or write to local chambers of commerce for information on places the family might visit and sites of special interest along the way.

| H16 | **Mapping a Virtual Trip** | Standards: 1, 3, 4, 7, 8, 12 |

Even the simplest maps display an incredible amount of information. You can read names of cities and states, places of special interest, mountain ranges, rivers, and much more. Parents and children can collaborate to estimate the distance between two points by looking at the map's key and taking note of the different-colored and different-shaped road signs that mark highways and interstates. They can explore an area's topography by understanding the various colors and symbols displayed on the map.

Technology provides many ways to learn about distance and travel. Students can access electronic informational sources on the Web to find maps and current weather information for most cities in the country. GPS (Global Positioning Satellite) devices can help families mark and relocate their favorite fishing hole or campsite or to calculate the distance between home and Grandma's house.

Have the students choose a location they would like to visit. Schedule a "virtual" trip using maps and information obtained from Internet sites. Have students plan a two week trip and mark the route using colored pens. Have them determine the number of miles they must cover in a day to reach their destination and identify interesting stops along the way.

133

| H17 | Make and Model | Standards: 1, 6 |

"What is the make and model of that car or truck?" Parents can motivate their child to read and write by playing a guessing game with them. Ask the child to guess the make and model of an approaching vehicle. The child confirms the guess by reading the name of the vehicle as it passes. A child can also write a list of the vehicles' names and track the number of each type of vehicle identified. Older children can write the names of the state from the vehicles' license plates. Encourage them to use each state's abbreviation on their list.

References

Behavior report. (n.d.). Retrieved July 30, 2001, from http://www.geocities.com/SoHo/Village/6305/behavior.html

National PTA (1998, May). *National standards for parent/family involvement programs.* Retrieved July 30, 2001, from http://www.pta.org/programs/pfistand.htm

Robinson, N. (1997). Working with families. In McCormick, L., Loeh, D. F., & Schiefelbusch, R. L., *Supporting children with communication difficulties in inclusive settings: School-based language intervention.* Boston: Allen & Bacon.

Roth, R. P., & Worthington, C. K. (1997). *Treatment resource manual for speech-language pathology.* San Diego, CA: Singular.

Communication Questionnaire

Student:		Date:
Team Member's Names:		

Circle a number on the scale that represents your feelings about the types of communication you would like to receive or the types of communication in which you would like to participate.

Type of Communication	Least				Most
written notes	1	2	3	4	5
e-mails	1	2	3	4	5
phone calls to home	1	2	3	4	5
phone calls to work	1	2	3	4	5
individual conferences at school	1	2	3	4	5
group conferences at school	1	2	3	4	5
regular notebook or journal entries	1	2	3	4	5
audio tapes	1	2	3	4	5
regular school progress reports	1	2	3	4	5
report cards	1	2	3	4	5

Other: _____

_____

_____

_____

Circle a number on the scale that represents your feelings about the types of information you would like to receive about your child.

Type of Information	Least				Most
behavior	1	2	3	4	5
organization	1	2	3	4	5
daily work	1	2	3	4	5
performance on quizzes and tests	1	2	3	4	5
special accomplishments	1	2	3	4	5
eating habits	1	2	3	4	5
taking medication	1	2	3	4	5

Other: _____

_____

_____

_____

Reinforcer Inventory

Name:	Date:

Circle the 10 activities you would like to do the most. After you have circled 10 activities, rank the importance of the the activities you chose from 1 to 10, with 1 being the most important and 10 being the least important.

	Take care of the class pet for the day and bring it home overnight.		Eat lunch with my favorite person.
	Be first in the bus line or sit in the front seat of the car on the way to school.		Earn weekly allowance for chores.
	Receive a "no homework" pass.		Choose the music on the car radio.
	Use the computer.		Surf the Internet.
	Get first pick of recess game.		Choose a movie or video to watch.
	Go to a friend's house for lunch.		Play a game with a friend.
	Play on an athletic team.		Do homework after dinner.
	Cook something for dinner.		Plan a weekend family trip.
	Select clothes to wear to school.		Stay after school to help teachers.
	Go to the library to select a book or book on tape.		Listen to radio or CD with headphones.

Note: Items can be added or deleted to better match the age of the student.

Tracking Chart

Tasks	M	T	W	Th	Fr	S	Su	M	T	W	Th	Fr	S	Su
Student:								Date:						
1. _____ _____														
2. _____ _____														
3. _____ _____														
4. _____ _____														
5. _____ _____														
6. _____ _____														
7. _____ _____														
8. _____ _____														

Reward: _____

_____

_____

_____

Consequences: _____

_____

_____

_____

Contract

Contract

I, _____, agree to _____

when _____

I understand that _____

_____
Name

_____
Name

_____
Date

Student:	Date:

Describe the behavior:. _____

_____

_____

_____

_____

Which rule was broken? _____

_____

_____

What are the consequences for breaking the rule? _____

_____

_____

What can you do so it won't happen again? _____

_____

_____

What will the consequences be for breaking the rule again? _____

_____

_____

Teacher:	Date:
Student:	Date:
Parent:	Date:

Activity	English Language Arts Standards											
	1	2	3	4	5	6	7	8	9	10	11	12
M1							X				X	X
M2								X				X
M3												X
M4								X			X	X
M5												X
M6							X					X
M7											X	X
M8												X
M9		X							X	X	X	X
M10												X
M11												X
M12									X	X	X	X
M13												X
L1			X									
L2			X			X						
L3			X			X						
L4			X			X						
L5			X			X						
L6			X			X						
L7			X			X						
L8			X			X						
L9		X	X	X	X	X	X	X	X	X	X	X
L10			X									
L11				X							X	X	
L12			X	X		X						X
L13		X		X		X			X	X		X

M=Chapter 2: Motivation, pages 13-26; L=Chapter 3: Listening and Speaking, pages 27-40

Activity	English Language Arts Standards											
	1	2	3	4	5	6	7	8	9	10	11	12
L14				X					X	X		X
L15				X								X
L16	X	X	X									
L17			X	X		X		X			X	
L18	X						X		X			X
L19	X		X	X	X	X					X	X
R1			X									
R2			X									
R3			X									
R4			X			X				X		
R5			X									
R6			X									
R7			X			X					X	
R8			X			X						
R9			X			X						
R10			X			X						
R11			X			X				X		
R12			X			X						
R13			X			X						
R14			X			X						
R15			X			X						
R16			X			X						
R17			X			X						
R18			X			X						
R19			X			X						
R20			X									

L=Chapter 3: Listening and Speaking, pages 27-40; **R**=Chapter 4: Reading, pages 41-66

Activity	English Language Arts Standards											
	1	2	3	4	5	6	7	8	9	10	11	12
R21			X			X	X					
R22			X			X						
R23	X	X	X			X			X	X	X	
R24	X		X								X	
R25			X							X		
R26			X	X								
R27			X						X		X	
R28			X									
R29			X			X						
R30	X	X	X			X						
R31			X			X					X	
R32			X			X					X	
R33		X	X			X					X	
R34		X	X			X				X		
R35			X			X						
R36			X									
R37		X	X									
R38	X	X	X									
R39	X	X	X									
R40	X	X	X	X								
R41	X	X	X	X								
R42	X	X	X	X								
R43		X	X			X						
R44	X	X	X	X							X	
R45	X	X	X					X				
R46	X	X	X	X	X	X			X	X	X	X
R47	X	X	X	X		X	X		X		X	

R=Chapter 4: Reading, pages 41-66

Activity	English Language Arts Standards											
	1	2	3	4	5	6	7	8	9	10	11	12
W1			X	X	X	X					X	
W2					X							
W3			X	X	X	X			X		X	
W4				X	X		X	X	X	X	X	
W5			X	X	X	X				X		X
W6					X		X	X				X
W7	X	X	X			X					X	
W8	X	X	X			X					X	
W9	X		X	X	X	X	X	X	X	X	X	X
W10				X								
W11				X								
W12				X								
W13				X								
W14			X	X	X	X			X	X		X
W15								X				
W16	X	X	X	X	X	X			X			
W17				X	X		X	X				X
W18					X	X						
W19				X	X				X		X	
W20				X	X				X		X	
W21				X	X	X						
W22				X	X	X						
W23			X	X	X	X						
W24				X	X	X		X	X		X	X

W=Chapter 5: Written Language, pages 67-84

Activity	English Language Arts Standards											
	1	2	3	4	5	6	7	8	9	10	11	12
C1				X				X				X
C2			X	X					X	X	X	
C3			X	X					X			
C4				X					X	X	X	X
C5	X		X			X		X		X		
C6			X									
C7	X		X									
C8	X		X									
C9	X		X									
C10	X		X									
C11	X		X									
C12				X			X	X			X	
C13		X	X	X			X			X		
C14	X		X									
C15	X		X				X		X	X	X	
C16			X									
C17			X	X			X				X	X
C18		X	X	X								
C19	X			X			X	X				
C20			X									
C21	X	X	X						X			
C22			X	X								
C23	X	X	X				X		X	X		
C24			X	X								

C=Chapter 6: Content Area Skills, pages 85-108

Activity	English Language Arts Standards											
	1	2	3	4	5	6	7	8	9	10	11	12
C25	X		X	X	X	X	X	X	X	X	X	
C26				X								
C27			X								X	
C28	X		X			X			X	X		
C29				X							X	
C30			X									
C31			X	X				X				
S1									X			X
S2									X			X
S3									X			X
S4							X		X			X
S5								X				X
S6	X			X								X
S7				X	X						X	X
S8				X								X
S9				X		X			X	X		X
S10					X	X	X	X			X	
S11				X					X			X
S12	X			X					X	X		X
S13				X	X				X			X
S14				X	X				X			X
S15				X	X							X
S16				X					X			X

C=Chapter 6: Content Area Skills, pages 85-108; **S**=Chapter 7: Social Skills, pages 109-120

Activity	English Language Arts Standards											
	1	2	3	4	5	6	7	8	9	10	11	12
H1		X			X				X	X	X	X
H2			X		X							X
H3			X	X				X			X	X
H4	X						X	X				X
H5								X				
H6			X	X								
H7			X	X								
H8				X				X				X
H9												X
H10			X	X								X
H11									X		X	X
H12				X					X	X	X	X
H13				X					X			
H14	X		X		X		X	X				X
H15	X		X		X		X	X				X
H16	X		X	X			X	X				X
H17	X					X						

H=Chapter 8: Home Activities, pages 121-140

19-02-987654321